Pray Your Care

OVERCOMING FEAR AND WALKING IN
THE FEAR OF THE LORD

Shirley Hernandez

TRILOGY CHRISTIAN PUBLISHERS
Tustin, CA

Trilogy Christian Publishers
A Wholly Owned Subsidiary of Trinity Broadcasting Network
2442 Michelle Drive
Tustin, CA 92780

Copyright © 2019 by Shirley Hernandez

All Scripture quotations, unless otherwise noted, taken from the New King James Version®. Copyright © 1982 by Thomas Nelson. Used by permission. All rights reserved.

Scriptures marked (NIV) are taken from THE HOLY BIBLE, NEW INTERNATIONAL VERSION®, NIV® Copyright © 1973, 1978, 1984, 2011 by Biblica, Inc.® Used by permission. All rights reserved worldwide.

All rights reserved, including the right to reproduce this book or portions thereof in any form whatsoever.

For information, address Trilogy Christian Publishing

Rights Department, 2442 Michelle Drive, Tustin, Ca 92780.

Trilogy Christian Publishing/ TBN and colophon are trademarks of Trinity Broadcasting Network.

For information about special discounts for bulk purchases, please contact Trilogy Christian Publishing.

Manufactured in the United States of America

Trilogy Disclaimer: The views and content expressed in this book are those of the author and may not necessarily reflect the views and doctrine of Trilogy Christian Publishing or the Trinity Broadcasting Network.

Cover image: Photo by Andrew Neel from Pexels

10 9 8 7 6 5 4 3 2 1

Library of Congress Cataloging-in-Publication Data is available.

ISBN 978-1-64088-751-0

ISBN 978-1-64088-752-7 (e-book)

Contents

Introduction vii
1. The Call to Know Him.. 1
2. Living to Work.. 9
3. Money is the Source of Discontentment 23
4. Fear of God or Fear of the Unknown 37
5. Higher Intervention..53
6. Understanding God's Love 60
7. Time in His Presence is an Investment of
   High Return..69
8. Motherhood is a Gift From God 87
9. A Command with a Promise 97
10. Becoming One... 107
11. Don't Worry, Don't Be Anxious, Don't Be Afraid ... 117
12. The Core of Life is Death............................... 129

To my daughter Rachel, God's most amazing gift and blessing in my life, whose love for books has inspired me to write leading me to see that true wisdom rests in knowledge.

To my husband Bernie whose love, patience, and support led me to find my calling in life. Thank you for believing in me and teaching me to fight my fears.

I love you both with all my heart!

Introduction

"...I will show you whom you should fear..." (Luke 12:5)

I became aware of God's presence in my life when I was still very young. I accepted Jesus into my life but He did not become the most important relationship I had. I read my Bible cover to cover without understanding it, I read it to say that I did, but I could not tell you one memorized scripture that meant something in my life. I made my confession of faith and I desired to know God, but the things of this world and the distractions of life prevented me from bearing fruit. I never got to know Him then, but He works over the passage of time. He called me into His fellowship, He took a hold of me, and He never let me go.

For many years, God was part of my life only on Sundays at church. I did not have much of a prayer life; my prayers where simply requests for the things I knew I couldn't do for myself. Decades went by from the time

God took a hold of me to the moment in time that I could really say "I know Him." His presence became stronger in my trials when I would call out to Him for help only to know that He was always there for me.

When I met my husband, I was attending a big church in NYC and I introduced him to God and to church. He had grown up knowing about God but he did not know Him personally. I am amazed how God works and how He sets people in specific places to fulfill His purpose in our lives.

There was an old lady, a devout believer, who used to live right across the hall from his apartment. He used to call her grandma since she was very close to his family and she truly became like one with her care and love for him. Every day, as he used to get off the elevator of his building, his God-given grandma was praying earnestly for him and his sister. My husband has memories of her calling out to God for protection and of his name being mentioned time and time again. I dare to believe that she was praying for God to take a hold of their lives since she had lost a grandson to drugs. He never thought much of her prayers; as a matter of fact, they probably didn't mean anything to him, but the Lord heard those prayers.

My husband's sister became a believer and eventually my husband did too when he met me. When I met his grandma, she was well advanced in years but there was a glow in her countenance, and you could sense and see her peace and joy in the Lord. She died days short of her one hundredth birthday, and she was one of the most beautiful people I ever met. Her inward beauty reflected and gave light to all those around her.

Years ago, after I started seeking God, I clearly heard in my spirit that I was to write a book on the fear of the Lord. I never understood how that was going to tie in with my life of fear at the time. One day, in my deepest need, I called out to God and I clearly heard in my spirit Luke 12:5. I could hardly wait to get home and read the scripture given to me and when I did, I realized that the Lord was showing me that the only fear that is worth having is the fear of Him. I had been trapped in my own fears for many years, and as I was learning to call out on His name, He began to lead me to study the fear of the Lord.

This new revelation led me to start writing my thoughts, my feelings, and the things that I was learning day by day. I have kept journals which became part of what I do for years and while journaling, I not only wrote what was happening in my life, but I wrote my prayers to God. As a matter of fact, I wrote letters to God. I have learned to pray by writing to Him.

My husband, who came to God when he met me and because of the prayers of an elderly woman, became the instrument that God would use not only to mold me into the woman that I needed to become to serve Him, but also to push me into my destiny. He believed in me more than I believed in myself. He not only loved me and stood by me when I was not lovable, but he also inspired me to become a better mother and a better wife.

The work that God wanted to do in me would require a broken and a submissive heart and it was not until I got to that point of surrender, that I began to see fruit in my life. I professed to have faith yet I was complaining about everything on a daily basis. I had lots of issues to overcome, especially fears and doubts that prevented me from growing spiritually. I was living in fear because I did not know the Lord. He would eventually lead me to learn that those who know Him fear Him, but those who don't know Him are in great fear.

In the pages to come, I will let you into the pages of my life. I will take you on a journey that God Himself took me to transform my thinking and my living. A journey that would lead me to this very moment in time when I can finally visualize the Lord's purpose for my life. After going through cycles of soul and spirit renovation, I believe that the Lord has called me to write for Him. It never crossed my mind that this is what I was called to do, but the work that He's been doing in my life will bear more fruit and much fruit when He is able to use me for His honor and glory.

Pray Your Care is a book about how prayer changes every aspect of our lives. It is about reaching out to God with the certainty that our prayers are answered because He is an all loving, caring, merciful God who takes pleasure in those who fear Him and desire to do His will. I used prayer to set me free from my afflictions and my fears. Praying and living in the fear of the Lord is the most rewarding experience in this life. It brings the peace of God that surpasses all understanding, and this in itself is priceless.

As you read this book, I hope you meditate on God's goodness and mercy toward you every single day. I believe that everything I have learned, every experience, and even every mistake, God is able to use for good in the life of anyone as He did on mine. No stage in our lives is ever wasted if we use it for His honor and glory. God has been my rock, my comfort, my hope, my healer, my provider, my peace and my strength. If He has done it for me, He can also do it for whosoever will chose to believe in Him. Allow Him to bless you, as He has and continues to bless me.

I will meditate on the glorious splendor of Your majesty, and on Your wondrous works. Men shall speak of the might of Your awesome acts, and I will declare Your greatness. They shall utter the memory of your great goodness, and shall sing of Your righteousness. They shall speak of the glory of Your kingdom, and talk of Your power, to make known to the sons of men His mighty acts, and the glorious majesty of His kingdom.

Psalm 145:5-7, 11-12

The Call to Know Him

"Get out of your country, from your family and from your father's house, to the land that I will show you" (Genesis 12:1).

I met my husband when we were in college. I still remember the day I saw him outside our campus, I thought to myself, *"He's cute. I wonder what his life is like."* I don't know why I had this thought, I only remember that a couple of months later, we were sitting in the same class, grouped together with other students and working on a project. Months later, I called him to see if he wanted to hang out, and we have been together ever since then.

When we got married, we got an apartment a couple of miles away from my parents. Shortly after that, they moved to their native country and my sister became part of our lives and space. She came to live with us on and off for the next couple of years. Eventually my parents moved back to the US and they moved in with us also. I can't recall us being alone much for the first years of our marriage because my family was always there. My biggest mistake was not setting boundaries in the beginning. Also, I did not have the respect that I owed my husband to let him be the head of our family and set the rules in our house. Anyone will go as far as you let them if you don't say "Enough!"

Eventually, after moving back and forth a couple of times, my parents retired and moved back to their native country, Bolivia. They have been visiting us every year ever since. I love to have them around, especially because my daughter gets to know them and they love her so much. I have also learned to appreciate them and respect them more over the years since the Lord taught me the true meaning of honoring my parents, something I will share later as you read. Here is something I wrote on one of their yearly visits:

My parents are staying with us on a summer vacation which doesn't seem to end. Today is the first day of my husband's short summer vacation which he took with the intention of us (including my parents) going on a short trip. I already know it's not going to happen, the reason? There is tension in the air. My husband can't wait for them to leave and my parents are not fond of him. I ask myself, "How is it that after more than twenty years of us being married, my parents cannot see my husband as a son and why?" I am in a position that I don't feel comfortable in. I feel split in between. I love my husband with all of my heart and I love my parents too.

I remember the time my parents came back to America after moving back to their native country, it all started with their idea to buy a house where we could all live in. At the time, we had only been married for a couple of years. They moved here furniture and all! We had started searching for a house, but in the process, we realized that we had too much credit card debt to make such a purchase. My mom got sick during that time knowing that this would never happen and she was in and out of hospitals all the time. We were crowded in our apartment and my dad could not work because he had to take care of her.

Their furniture was to arrive in four short months and my husband thought they would put it in storage; but when it did, they asked me if they could have it in our apartment, of course I never consulted with my husband and I said yes. They piled all the boxes of furniture in our living room making a wall of separation between them and us. We no longer had a nice apartment but a storage room.

A couple of months later we found out that my sister was having problems with her husband and she was pregnant with her third child who was about to be born. She also came to live with us, and the baby was born in NYC. What was I thinking?

Not only did we have my parents in our apartment but now we had my sister and her baby!

Looking back, it was all wrong. I was being influenced by my family who were thinking only about themselves! I never saw it this way but my husband did and I never listened. I don't hold my parents or my sister responsible for any of this, I allowed it to happen. I let them into our lives and put no boundaries; I let them get as far as they wanted to.

My husband has always been a wonderful, caring man. We have had our ups and downs in our marriage, but we always managed to stay by each other's side. Most arguments were based on disagreements due to my resistance to submit as a wife. When we got married, I allowed my parents and my sister's lives to interfere with my decisions. I failed to see that I was becoming extremely involved in their lives.

One of my fears has always been to hurt my parents' feelings. I have come a long way but I'm still working on it. As for my sister, I realized that I let her life become a part of mine right after I got married. I've always had a sincere desire to help her; my mistake was to let her difficulties affect my emotions and wear me out. I saw myself responsible for her and I wasn't; she is my sister and I always loved her very much, but I learned that I cannot fix everything for anyone. I have to step back and let God do His work. Setting boundaries is the right thing do, even when it comes to family.

Five years into our marriage, we decided to build a new house in a nice development in the middle of the sunshine state, and as soon it was finished, my husband suggested we move right away into our newly constructed house. We had no jobs in perspective but that didn't stop us. At the time, we only had each other and our dog and we thought, "How hard could it possibly be to find jobs and start a life there?" Without second thoughts, we quit our jobs and we moved. We were in for an adventure that would change our lives.

My dad, who at the time was in his native country, decided to join us in Florida shortly after we arrived. He got himself a car and a job and decided that he was going to stay with us. Our time in Florida was short, we lived there for eight short months during which we never found good paying jobs, and we got hit by three major hurricanes. We completely ran out of resources and realized that we could no longer live with salaries that did not fully cover our essential expenses. We were living each day with the hope that things would change, but nothing ever changed. Sooner or later we had to decide on what was best for us.

During our stay in Florida we sought the Lord on and off, but He never became our top priority. We never saw

Him as being part of our lives, we did not know that He desires to be involved in every aspect of our lives. Even then, He was directing our steps as we failed to notice the work He was doing in our lives. I now see how He was using this time of uncertainty to prepare us for the future. He trains us in every stage of our lives for what will come down the road, I found this to be a pattern of God. Everything happens for a reason and no season is wasted.

   Early in the spring of the following year, we decided to sell and move back to NYC. We listed our house and sold it very quickly making a very nice profit on it. This was no coincidence; this was the hand of God. It worked out to be a flip. We never planned things to happen this way, but everything we learned from it was worth the time we put into it.

We may plan all we want but at the end of the day, God will take us to where we are supposed to be. He works to accomplish His will in our lives no matter where we are, He directs our steps. It took me a long time to understand this, but I finally get it; the Lord works in ways we don't always understand. He is always there for us and we often miss Him because we are too busy mapping out our own lives, not realizing that He's already done it for us.

My mom joined us before we moved to NYC. We did not have any jobs in perspective and no place of our own to move to. My parents moved into a hotel and my husband and I into my mother-in-law's apartment, we lived with her for six months. During this time, we got jobs, purchased an apartment and got back to our routine of work and life. We were actually better off than when we left, we were able to pay off our debts and we felt more confident about the future because the Lord had been good to us.

We lived in our new apartment until we found out I was pregnant. My parents moved into our building into an apartment across the hall from us. The Lord allowed it to happen this way, I know it deep inside my heart. I was glad to have them close, but my husband did not see us raising a family in an apartment, as he always longed for more room away from the city. He had grown up in the city and he did not like it, he wanted a house, a backyard, but most of all he wanted privacy. I see it now.

My husband was tired of having my family around all the time and God saw his heart. His main priority has always been to make me happy, but his patience has been tested time and time again. Only the unfailing love of God our Father, lots of prayer, and the love and commitment that we have for each other has kept us strong in every stage of our lives.

We had to leave New York, but most of all we had to leave my family and their effect in my life if our marriage was to survive. God never failed to show Himself strong for us, He was directing our steps. We were about to go on a journey to find out how faithful He truly was and to know how much He loved and cared for us.

Just as God commanded Abraham to move to the promised land leaving behind his family, He led us into a new land, a place where He wanted to work in us away from family, distractions, and everything that was hindering our spiritual growth. I was afraid of hurting my family's feelings and I was afraid of what other people thought about me. My fears were many because I did not know God, I was more concerned about material things than investing in my spiritual life.

In our new home we would learn to seek the face of God, ask for his help, learn how to pray and be led by the Spirit of God to know Him and to learn the fear of the Lord.

Hear my cry, O God; attend to my prayer. From the end of the earth I will cry to You, when my heart is overwhelmed; lead me to the rock that is higher than I.

Psalm 61:1-2

2

Living to Work

"Do not work for the food that spoils, but for food that endures to eternal life, which the Son of Man will give you" (John 6:27 NIV).

Months before I got pregnant, we had the desire to have a vacation house away from the city. My husband researched an area in Connecticut where we could afford to buy a house to get away to during weekends and holidays. We got a real estate agent and saw probably a dozen houses before we narrowed it down to the very house we would buy and move into just within a year. There are no coincidences with God; He was preparing us all along for our big move.

When we found out I was pregnant, I was caught by surprise. We might not have planned it, but God certainly did. I had been pregnant twice before and both pregnancies ended in miscarriages, so because of this, there was a deep level of fear in me. I was afraid to go through the pain and disappointment, but God had other plans for us. This was going to be a successful pregnancy. I was going to have this child all to the honor and glory of God.

What happened next was in such orderly fashion that only God could have orchestrated the events that took place in the months to come. Within weeks of discovering my pregnancy, I found myself out of a job. My husband, who was always looking for change and better opportunities, got a new job in Connecticut, the state we would eventually move into in just a matter of months. All of a sudden, everything lined up for us to move. Little did I know that God was directing our steps to move to the place of our encounter, the place in which we would discover who truly was the head of the household, the head of the family and the one true provider.

We put our apartment on the market and sold it right away. At the time, I couldn't understand or see what I know now. I remember the day we got an offer, I told my husband that I did not want to move. I was afraid of the unknown. I wanted to stay and live close to my parents. I was being difficult and I was not submitting to my husband's decision to move, a decision we both agreed on. What I failed to see was that the Lord was leading us to accomplish His will.

God had a destiny and a plan for our lives all along, but it would take time and discipline to prune all the rough edges. He had to teach me to let go of my fears. I was afraid of change. I liked stability. I felt protected knowing that my family was around me if I needed anything. But I was about to learn that being led by the Spirit of God is living day by day trusting in Him. It was a battle to let go and let God do His will in our lives. It would have been much easier to surrender it all and say,

"Lord, do as you please, I trust you, I surrender my will, I give you my fears, my concerns, my doubts. Take my life and mold it to your honor and glory. I don't know what the future holds, but I know who holds the future. You are the potter, I am the clay, do your work in me. I will not resist to your good plans because I know you love me, and I will trust you in everything because I know that your thoughts are higher than mine, and they are for good and not evil."

We purchased a house one hundred miles away from New York City. I was in a new house, in a new neighborhood, with a newborn child and my husband quit his new job in Connecticut. He was asked to travel overseas and I could not picture us away from him. I needed him near. I did not foresee the financial difficulties that we would have to face as a result of it, but I believed that we were better together than financially well off and far apart. Regardless of everything that came after, this was one decision that I never regretted.

We lived on the profit that we made from the sale of our apartment for six months, and after seeking another job all along, he found a job in retail that paid him very little. We did not know that in that setting he was going to learn to depend on God and rely on Him. This would take years of frustration and headaches.

My parents, not happy with our move, reminded me every day that it was a mistake to move so far away. They used to blame my husband for taking me far away from them. I was having many sleepless nights and many doubts clouded my mind. My stress level intensified as I was starting to become hopeless with our situation. This was the beginning of our arguments and financial conflicts. It was during this period of our lives that we started saying things to each other that were very hurtful and uncalled for. Our financial situation brought out the worst in us.

Frustrated and overwhelmed, blinded by fear and depression, I decided to get a part-time job in NYC shortly after my husband got his. I don't remember for a moment asking his opinion on the matter. It was my decision and I was going to do what I thought was necessary at the moment. He didn't have a say in it and even if he did, I would not listen! My will was to prevail regardless of what his thoughts were. I was set in doing what I thought was best for us.

The truth is that God's will was in none of my thoughts. I did not know that He orders our steps. I did not know that in order for me to achieve the level of peace and security that I wanted to have, I had to surrender my will to His. I did not realize that God was working in me and for me so that one day I would give Him the glory for all the things that He taught me along the way.

Not only was I back in the city, back to my family, but I was also back to the same job I left before our move to Florida. It was as if I wanted to go back to the past, or rather not let go of it. Everything pulled me back to what once was, only this time I was going against God's will.

I started working two days a week usually on weekends. I would have to go into the city the night before to drop off my daughter with my parents who were not so thrilled about taking care of her. For years I despised my mother because she did not want to watch my daughter while I worked. I was bitter and angry. I could not believe that my own mother would not want to watch my only child.

Was God hardening her heart? I never saw it this way, but now I do. There were signs all along which I never saw. My daughter used to cry every time I went to work because she did not want to let go of me. I had no peace; something didn't feel right about the whole situation. It felt like I was trying to walk against the wind. It never crossed my mind that God was trying to direct my eyes to look up and not at my own efforts. I was depending on my family to make things work. He led us out into a different land and there I was, back to everything I walked away from, and this time I was bringing my daughter into the equation.

My mind was cluttered with worry, fear, and desperation of not having my way. I made my own plans with the hope that things would work out just right. I did not consider that my plans without God in it were futile. He was not going to bless what He didn't approve. Yet even then, I know He was with me.

I remember the day I asked my mom to babysit on New Year's Eve so I could work, she said no because her schedule was full and it was out of the question. I took it the wrong way and I stormed out of her apartment frantic and distressed. All I could see was her hostility and selfishness that I did not see what God was trying to show me. It didn't cross my mind to pause and think about my situation. Maybe I was not supposed to work so far away, leaving my daughter to her care. Everything was against it; but even then, I did not give up. It was a huge mistake that I didn't see for years down the road.

Bitter, angry, and frustrated, I went around talking bad about my mother to everyone I knew. I was a victim of my own circumstances because I could not have my own way. I used to walk around crying all the time because in my eyes, I had a heartless mother who did not love me nor wanted to help me.

Since I found so much opposition, I opted to work on the days that my husband was off from work and I left my daughter to his care instead of my mom's. Willing to make anything work, I would have to commute over five hours a day just to make ends meet. There was no communication between us. I didn't see the big picture or God in it. All I could see was the big pile of bills we couldn't pay and the lack of things I wish I had. I took it upon myself to become the head of our family. I neglected to see that there was more to life than bills and work.

The days that I went to work seemed longer because I had to get up very early and come home very late at night. Hungry and tired, I used to walk into my kitchen where the dishes were piled up in the sink. I couldn't find one clean cup to use and it used to make me so angry. I would get very upset with my husband who had been home all day. *Poor me, I had to come home to such a mess*, I thought, and I would go upstairs and wake him up and nag him about the mess he left for me to clean up. I was very mean to him. I judged him and I even called him lazy. We used to argue, but after all was said, the following week things would be the same with no change.

I was very quick to observe the chores that my husband did not complete, but I failed to see that he was trying his best to take care of our daughter who was only a toddler at the time. He kept her entertained any way he could. His routine was to take her to the park to play with children her age, the library, the bookstore, and to other activities. I came home to fight with him about everything in the house he did not do, yet I never said a word to thank him for the great job he was doing as a dad.

When I see all the pictures and videos he made while caring for our daughter, I realize that my daughter was enjoying her time with her daddy. He captured and enjoyed the best memories of her childhood, while I was busy living to work and complaining about everything. My priorities were all wrong.

My daughter learned to love books and reading because her daddy invested his time reading to her, teaching her to read and bonding with her. I never cared to read, and books were not in my list of interests. What I did not know is that that years down the road, my daughter's love for books and reading would inspire me to read books like I never read before and today, I am writing this book because reading God's word led me to write and accomplish His will. Do you see how God works?

I heard many times that life is ten percent what happens to you and ninety percent how you react to it. I was so angry and blinded by my own bitterness; my reactions were all wrong because my heart was not right with God or with my husband. I was being judgmental and I wanted to look like a victim of my circumstances at the expense of making my husband and my mother look bad in front of others.

I wanted to look good in front of people. I think we all do, more so in front of outsiders. Sometimes, it is easy to pretend we live perfect lives. What I had yet to learn is that God is more interested in how I treat those closest to me when the doors are closed and when no one watching. He wants me to live in front of Him because that is exactly how I am at all times. He is always watching me; there are no walls of separation and no place to hide. My thoughts are known by Him even before they come to my mind. All things are naked and open to the eyes of Him to whom we must give an account. (Hebrews 4:13)

In the Old Testament the Israelites complained all the time. They complained about the food they didn't have and the food that they had too much of. Nothing made them happy. This was the reason God kept them wandering for forty long years in the wilderness. He was angered by their faithless actions and complaints. I was living in my own wilderness those days, and there seemed to be no way out of it. I was complaining about all my misfortunes and the things I did not have. I had a "poor me" mentality, running around the same mountain for years because I did not stop to look and see that my fear of not having enough had taken a hold of me.

Perhaps it was a period to evaluate and see what we did have instead of focusing on the things that I desired to have. I had a husband who loved me and our beautiful daughter. We were healthy and we also had a house and food. What else did we need? We needed God. We were relying on our jobs to take care of us and not on God who could have supplied all of our needs abundantly had we asked for it and submitted to His will.

As I write, I realized that my husband seems to have been silent in all this, but he wasn't. He was talking but I was not listening. Whatever he was saying was going in one ear and out the other. We were like two strangers living in the same house. I did not listen to him at all. I was stubborn and self-righteous. I thought I knew better than him. I thought that if he was not bringing in a big paycheck, I had to take charge of things. I could not look at the future because my spiritual eyes were tainted. All I saw was a dark present that I did not like, and deep inside, I was terrified.

I went through the same mountain of self-effort for years without seeing any improvement or results. When I realized that things were not getting better but worse, I learned to seek God. Problems, lack of resources, stress, depression, and health issues are all what drove me to seek God day after day, week after week and year after year.

I can't fix what happened in the past, I can only use what I have learned to have a better future. I was trying to rely on my own works, big mistake! I could've prayed more and worried less, but God was not part of my life then as He is now. I did not know any better because I did not know Him. I was afraid of everything and of everyone. I felt helpless and trapped in my fears.

Everything that happened during those dark, long days had to happen in order to get me to submit to God and make Him the Lord of my life. Yet even then, the Lord was leading me to prophesy that those days were to pass and that better times would come. Here is one of the first letters I wrote to God:

Lord, help me to stay focused on my goals. Help me to look at you and not at the adversities of this world. Help me to look at the beautiful things you gave me like my little daughter, to look at her innocence, her desire to live and to be happy every day, and her desire to wake up every morning when the sun comes out. Help me to look at nature, at animals... the beauty of your presence is in every flower in every tree, in the way the birds sing every morning.

Lord, you provide for all nature, so provide the same way for us. Help me to get close to You to become everything you want me to be. Put the desire in my heart to be like You, not to deceive myself, but to become as close to perfection as I can be. Erase all the bad thoughts in my head, and bring positive and beautiful thoughts to my mind. Help me to think that tomorrow will be a better day, that things are not always going to be the way they are now. These days shall pass and tomorrow shall be a brighter, better, and more prosperous day!

Give me the strength to hold on to your promises. You came that we might have life and have it abundantly. I love you my Lord, more than anything, you are my father and my creator. I have a little one, I know what love is all about. How much more must You love me. You have carried me every day of my life, will you please give me a better life now? Won't you please set me free from living day by day feeling like I'm not accomplishing anything. Renew every part of my body. Renew my mind and my spirit. Help me to become like You. Show me that You will always walk by my side, hand in hand. Help me, give me peace, give me joy, I'm your child...

As I felt like nothing was happening in my life and as the days, weeks, and even the years were endless and filled with the cares of life, the Lord was doing His work in me. He was transforming my heart and mind so that one day I would give Him the glory for His work in me.

> *Unless the Lord builds the house, those who build it labor in vain. Unless the lord guards the city, the guard keeps watch in vain. It is vain that you rise up early, and go late to rest, eating the bread of anxious toil; for he gives sleep to his beloved.*
> *Psalm 127:1-2 (NRSV)*

SHIRLEY HERNANDEZ

3

Money is the Source of Discontentment

"For where your treasure is, there your heart will be also."
(Luke 12:34)

Lack of resources was not always an issue in our lives. Things took a sharp turn once we moved to Connecticut. The first years of our marriage, I wasn't concerned about money at all. We both worked and we earned decent salaries, perhaps even more than enough to spend as we liked. It is easy to live happy and worry free when all is going well. It is also easy to forget to acknowledge God in the midst of it all. Yes, we know He is always there, but we are not so eager to seek Him because we think we can handle all things on our own. Somehow, we forget that God is in charge of our steps and nothing happens without Him.

I had always been in charge of our finances since the beginning. I do not know how that came about, I think it just happened. As a child and while living with my grandparents, I remember seeing my grandfather bring home his paycheck to my grandmother and she would dispose of the money as she needed. I liked this idea because, as a housewife, she always knew what was needed in the house. I know wives who handle their finances better than their husbands would ever do it, as my grandmother did. In my case, the fear of not having money to buy the next thing was my greatest challenge. Unfortunately, I made a series of mistakes not knowing how to enjoy the things that God gave us so freely to enjoy. God's idea for marriage is that the man is to be the head of the household. Perhaps if my husband would've been in charge of our finances since the beginning, things would've been different.

The fear of not having enough became my burden for years, and the devil took advantage of it. I was terrified at the thought of not knowing how we were going to pay for our bills, our gas, and our food. Every time I had a need, I used to call my parents crying to ask them for money, and I used to hate every minute of it. I felt terrible asking them for anything. I hated their pity and I thought I was being looked down on. Perhaps this feeling was only my perception, but it was the impression I got when I spoke to them. I put myself in such a position because I didn't even consult with my husband to make the calls. For years I had the same mentality: counting on my parents to help us meet our needs and putting my trust in the wrong source. My husband was not as troubled as I was regarding all the unpaid bills. Perhaps he had more faith than I did. His response was always the same, "They'll have to wait." We were not paying bills on time but we never went hungry or lacked our basic needs. The Lord always provided.

I used to get several phone calls from creditors who wanted their payments the same day. Feeling extremely anxious and completely helpless, I was scared to talk to them. I recall the day I called the bank regarding an extension on our car payments and I spoke to a woman who intimidated me, she told me that they needed a payment right away in order to avoid repossession. I panicked! I did not know what to do. The thought of not having a car to drive drove me crazy. But even then, in my fear, in my desperation, in my unbelief, God was working for us.

Right after my conversation with her, my mother-in-law called me to say that she had won money playing daily numbers and she wanted to deposit funds into our account. What were the chances of her calling me precisely at the hour of my deepest need and to tell me that she wanted to give us the money that we needed? Was it a coincidence? Of course not. The Lord did not test me beyond what I could bear. He saw my heart and He had mercy on me. There are no coincidences with God.

After I hung up the phone with my mother-in-law, I sobbed with a grateful heart for His faithfulness. It felt as if He was letting me know that He was still in control of all things and He was good and merciful toward me, even when my faith failed.

I was scared of not having enough and afraid of putting my trust in mere mortals. I was not submitting nor obeying my husband and I was avoiding the real issue which was my wrong thinking. If our lives were going to change for the better, I needed to start looking up to God and stop putting my trust and confidence elsewhere. I needed to renew my mind and let God do His work in my life.

I was seeking God and I was reading my Bible but I was not applying it into my life. True wisdom is applying the knowledge we acquire into our lives, transferring it from our heads to our hearts and living it out. I was not doing that, and for that reason I felt frustrated and overwhelmed. I did not want to pretend any more in front of everyone that all was well when it really wasn't. My husband and I were fighting almost every day. He used to get migraine headaches all the time because of our arguments due to our finances. Stress was causing me stomach problems and other health issues. Something needed to change.

I literally wasted years of my life being anxious and worried over things I had no control over. The devil had me wrapped up living in fear worried about everything: mortgage payments, car payments, food, transportation, etc., and it was all on my shoulders! I wanted to have the control of all things, but I had to change that and the sooner the better. At some point, I had to learn to apply God's word into my life, otherwise I was just reading scripture and it was not going to profit me at all.

> *"...everyone who hears these words of Mine and puts them into practice is like a wise man who built his house on the rock. The rain came down, the streams rose, and the winds blew and beat against that house; yet it did not fall, because it had its foundation on the rock. But everyone who hears these words of Mine and does not put them into practice is like a foolish man who build his house on the sand. The rain came down, the streams rose, and the winds blew and beat against that house, and it fell with a great crash."*
> Matthew 7:24-27 (NIV)

It was time to let go of the weight and burden of handling the finances all by myself. I wanted my husband to take the responsibility, but it was hard to let go of the control I had over the decisions in our household. First my attitude had to change, and that was not an easy task. When you think you know it all and you know it better than your spouse, conflicts arise. I was set in my old ways and that was something that needed to change in me.

Living by faith is walking by God's leading one step at a time, one day at a time. We don't always have to know everything. He gives us just enough wisdom for what we can handle at the moment. The trust we deposit in Him is the key to success. The hard part for me was submitting it all and obeying Him wholeheartedly.

> "Bring the full tenth into the storehouse so that there may be food in My house. Test Me in this way," says the Lord of Hosts. "See if I will not open the floodgates of heaven and pour out a blessing for you without measure."
>
> *Malachi 3:10 (HCSB)*

One of the most important things that we needed to learn as a family is that we must give in order to receive. Tithing was out of the question for us because we barely had enough to cover our expenses. We could not see ourselves being able to give one tenth of our income to our church. Regardless of the many teachings of the pastor on this subject, we simply couldn't get ourselves to do it.

Seeing that our financial situation was not changing and that we always had a lack of resources, we decided to try this new concept slowly. We used to give our tithe when we pushed ourselves to do it, but if we saw bills first, then we would give only what we had leftover. Not the right approach when it comes to faith and God, but you live and learn. The Bible says, "Give and it will be given to you. A good measure, pressed down, shaken together and running over, will be poured into your lap" (Luke 6:38 NIV).

We were giving to the Lord out of fear of not having enough and we did not see much change in our lives. We were getting by, but we needed to fully trust Him and to let go of the money that He entrusted into our lives. Years later and when we got enough wisdom to understand that He comes first in our lives and in our finances, we started tithing first. Before we paid for anything, our first ten percent was and is continually for the Lord. The Lord has taught us to set our priorities straight and to put Him first in our lives.

As wisdom got into my heart and when I learned that God owns it all, including the very next breath of my life, I realized that everything I have is a gift from Him, therefore I learned to disconnect myself from the love of money and I learned to trust Him for provision. You haven't learned anything until you apply what you have learned. When we started giving a portion of what belongs to the Lord, we were acknowledging that He is in charge of everything, not us. Giving helped us to trust in Him for provision. Somehow, our ninety percent goes further than a hundred percent without His blessing.

Little by little and applying all that I had learned about money and tithing, the cares of life, the mountain of bills that stole my joy for years, plus the desire to have things that I couldn't acquire and the bitterness that went along with it, started to fade one by one. Money became less important to me because I put God first in my life. His word says that if we seek Him first, then all those things which we chase after will come along because He knows our needs.

> *But seek first His kingdom and His righteousness, and all these things will be given to you as well. Therefore, do not worry about tomorrow,*

for tomorrow will worry about itself. Each day has enough trouble of its own.
Matthew 6:33-34 (NIV)

I needed to learn to give God first place in my life; not money, not things, not possessions, nor anything, nor anyone. When God becomes number one, everything else falls into its place. He leaves no room for any other gods, and nothing or no one will take His place because He designed it to be this way.

We started our walk with God with major debt, credit cards, backed-up mortgage, car payments, and taxes. We were completely saturated with bills coming from every direction, but for years, taxes got the best of us. My husband used to do our tax returns every year and somehow, we owed thousands of dollars in back taxes, both state and federal. We later found out that he was claiming the maximum number of exemptions in order to get more money every paycheck, a huge mistake that cost us lots more money to fix. Immediate gratification costs more in the long run. The numbers only kept growing every year and I did not see how we could ever get rid of such a debt.

Slowly but steadily, we started coming out of debt. The income tax debt vanished completely over the course of time; it took time and patience, but it was as if the Lord shortened the time it took to clear itself out. We no longer owed money in taxes, but we were actually getting money back when doing our taxes which never happened before. We also learned to pay cash for our necessities. It makes a huge difference when you don't spend what you don't have, you learn to value what you do have and not waste it on things you don't even need.

God's law of first fruits works, otherwise He would not ask us to tithe, because whatever He asks us to do is for our benefit and to receive blessings from Him.

"Give, and it will be given to you; good measure, pressed down, shaken together, and running over will be put into your bosom" (Luke 6:38).

Change took time, patience, and prayer. It did not happen overnight. We went through lots of tests and trials in our finances to finally understand that the One who provides is God alone. I had to have a brainwash and erase the lies of the enemy. Instead, I needed to fill my mind with the promises of God. It all begins with a new mind-set and the determination to fight the enemy every day.

I have learned to ask in order to receive. Because of prayer, my life is simpler because I ask God for what I need and I surrender everything else I have no control of. Anxiety only causes me stress and this does not come from God. His peace only comes when I willingly and completely cast my cares on Him. Then and only then can I experience the peace that surpasses all understanding.

You don't learn to depend on God unless you have been put through trial after trial where your faith is tested and God proves Himself faithful. We learned to trust Him during those trials. What used to be the cause of our fights and conflicts turned into our praise and worship of the One Provider. The very thing that caused me stress and anger became my stepping stone into the next level of trust and dependence on the Lord.

Journal notes:

This past week has been historic, and once again I saw the hand of God in our lives. Last week this day, I didn't know how we would make ends meet. We had no money and as I kept praying, the Lord provided every single day. I kept this scripture throughout the week:

"I have been young and now am old, yet I have not seen the righteous forsaken, nor his descendants begging for bread" (Psalm 37:25).

This was a constant reminder to me that God is in control of all things, and He was! We lacked no food, no gas, no anything! He provided every single day!

Thank you, Father! You are an awesome God! You are to be praised every day of our lives, for with You is our hope and our life. You are our provider. You make rivers in the desert. You are our God and our fortress. Thank you!

I still remember like yesterday the day my husband said, "Storms may come and go, but we are standing on our rock and we will not be moved." I have learned that you cannot make such a statement unless you have a certain level of maturity and much trust in the Lord. You cannot profess such faith unless you know the One Provider who never fails.

As I look back and over the course of the years that went by, I learned to trust God and not worry. Was it easy? Not at all! It is easier said than done. Fear pops up when I least expect it, because the devil is constantly working to tempt me into going back to my old ways. My husband keeps me in line reminding me that we serve an Almighty God who works in our lives to help us acquire dependency only in Him. I don't think much transformation would've taken place in my life had it not been for my husband's constant reminders and reprimands to stand firm on my faith and not listen to the lies of the enemy, but to rely only on God for our every need.

God made us stewards of all that we have. One day we may have plenty of money to buy all we need and want, and the next we may have none at all; even then, we give glory to God no matter what. In much and in little, in abundance and in need, true contentment comes from the Lord and from our relationship to Him, not from money.

I don't know what your needs are, but I can tell you that God is an awesome God. He is faithful and full of compassion. He is found when we seek him with all our heart. Sometimes we wait to call out to Him in our deepest need, when we see no other way out, but it doesn't have to be this way. Do not wait to call out on Him, don't let another day pass you by without having the joy and the peace that only He offers to those who will put their trust in Him. He is near to all those who call upon His name. Pray your care and watch Him work in your life.

> *I have learned to be content whatever the circumstances. I know what it is to be in need, and I know what it is to have plenty. I have learned the secret of being content in any and every situation, whether well fed or hungry, whether living*

in plenty or in want. I can do all things through Him who gives me strength.

Philippians 4:11-13 (NIV)

Fear of God or Fear of the Unknown

"...do not fear what they fear and do not dread it. The Lord Almighty is the one you are to regard as holy, He is the One you are to fear, He is the one you are to dread"
(Isaiah 8:12-13 NIV).

Those long drives from New York to Connecticut very late at night gave me the chance to talk to God about all the things that concerned me and I often prayed for protection as I was driving. I didn't always drive all the way to work, sometimes I drove half-way and I took the train into the city since it was easier and there was less traffic to deal with. One night, I got off the train to get into my car to find out that I had a flat tire. I had to call the insurance company late at night to send someone to change it for me. I had to wait in the car until someone was dispatched to help me. Another time, because of a similar incident, I came home at three in the morning to sleep for two hours because the next morning I had to go back to work.

I knew that I had willpower and determination the day that I had to walk very far to the adjacent parking lot to get to my car. Walking through a deserted parking lot, then through a deserted street and into the darkest parking lot which was across the street from a cemetery, was the most terrifying thing I have ever done.

On another instance, I left work late and I had to drive all the way home. There was always traffic getting out of the city no matter what time of night it was. I was so tired that night that I had to pray, talk to myself, and open the windows of the car so I could stay awake. I never felt so sleepy as I did then, but the Lord kept me awake and safe even then.

Looking back, I was risking my life doing what I thought was necessary for us to survive. I neglected to see the dangers that I was exposing myself to, but God was with me all along. I wanted to have control of all things and drive the direction in my life. However, nothing slipped by Him. His hand of protection was always upon me, He was merciful and full of compassion toward me. He put a shield of protection upon me and

He sent His angels to protect me because His love for His children is greater than anything else.

One night, as I found myself troubled and scared of a situation I was in with a debt collector, I called out to God in fear and desperation of not being able to do anything on my own, and He gave me a scripture. In my spirit, I heard Luke 12:5 and I remember that I couldn't wait to get home to open my Bible and see what it said. When I got home I read,

> "But I will show you whom you should fear, fear Him who, after He has killed, has power to cast into hell; yes, I say to you, fear Him!"

This scripture was a defining moment in my life because I knew that it came from the mouth of God and it was meant for me. He was teaching me to fear Him before anyone else. I was living in fear like a scared child in the midst of darkness and I had to find a switch to turn on the light in me and stop being scared of people and everything else. I knew then that the Lord was answering my questions and my prayers with scripture, so I began to read the Bible on a daily basis and under a new light. I started little by little with a new approach that was not the same as of years before. I was not looking to read the Bible just to read it; it became my daily bread. I wanted to feed my spirit and my soul and my desire to know God increased every day. I did not want religion, I wanted God. I was tired of living defeated and hopeless. This was not the life that Jesus died for me to have.

Reading scripture helped me understand that David's closeness to God was in his connection to Him. He acknowledged that there was a force bigger and greater than anything in the world. When David saw that the Philistines had Goliath to fight for them, David understood that his God was bigger than any giant threatening to defeat God's people. In fact, David never called Goliath a giant, he referred to him as the uncircumcised philistine. David knew that his God was capable of defeating all giants; He had done it for him in the past. He had delivered him from the lion and from the bear, and of course He was going to deliver him from Goliath. His faith was so great that he had no doubts, only faith and confidence. Because of this great faith, he was able to defeat the Philistines' giant with a sling and a stone.

David's faith inspired me to look at God with the same eyes he did. I had to learn to trust Him. David knew God and had a relationship with Him, he knew the fear of God, and he was aware that outside of himself, he could do nothing. This is the God that I wanted to serve.

When an opportunity arose to celebrate my daughter's birthday in Disney, and knowing that we would have to fly, I prayed to God for months in advance. I was terrified to get on an airplane. Just the thought of it made me extremely anxious. One day while sitting in the presence of the Lord, I learned that those who know the Lord fear Him, but those who don't know Him are in great fear.

Isn't the fear of flying a fear of dying also? I had to learn to understand that my life is in the hands of God. I always desired to be in control of all things, but one thing I cannot and I will never be in control of is the length of my life. It was crucial for me to let go of the fear of dying and trust in the Lord; after all, nothing is over until God says it is, so why fear?

Working to overcome all the fears that were not letting me live free and confident in the Lord, I found a scripture that helped me let go of those fears:

> *Now since the children have flesh and blood in common, Jesus also shared in these, so that through His death He might destroy the one holding the power of death- that is the devil- and free those who were held in slavery all their lives by the fear of death.*
>
> *Hebrews 2:14-15 (CSB)*

I had to overcome my fear of flying and understand that nothing is out of God's control. He holds my life in the palm of His hand. When I got on that plane to go on our vacation, my faith was bigger than any fears I might have had in the past. I was confident, secure, and fully assured that no matter what, I was with God and He with me.

As we go on a quest to know Him more, there is less fear of people and other things. As we begin to reach out to God with a humble heart and a submissive spirit, we acquire a reverential fear of Him. It is a respect. It is the knowledge that He is all powerful and that He is in control of our lives. We are His sheep and He is our Shepherd.

As I began to study verses in the Bible on the fear of the Lord, I kept coming back to Psalm 34. I read it, memorized it, and meditated on it. It has changed my whole outlook on life. The first time I heard it was in church when we were going through financial turmoil. A guest speaker came to preach on it and I will never forget that it touched my life in a very special way on a day that I needed it most.

> *I sought the Lord, and He heard me, and delivered me from all my fears. They looked to Him and were radiant, and their faces were not*

ashamed. This poor man cried out, and the Lord heard him, and saved him out of all his troubles. The angel of the Lord encamps around those who fear Him, and delivers them. Oh, taste and see that the Lord is good; blessed is the man who trusts in Him!

Oh, fear the Lord, you His saints! There is no want to those who fear Him. The young lions lack and suffer hunger; but those who seek the Lord shall not lack any good thing. Come, you children, listen to me; I will teach you the fear of the Lord. Who is the man who desires life, and loves many days, that he may see good?
Keep your tongue from evil, and your lips from speaking deceit. Depart from evil and do good; seek peace and pursue it. The eyes of the Lord are on the righteous, and His ears are open to their cry.

The face of the Lord is against those who do evil, to cut off the remembrance of them from the earth. The righteous cry out, and the Lord hears and delivers them out of all their troubles. The Lord is near to those who have a broken heart, and saves such as have a contrite spirit. Many are the afflictions of the righteous, but the Lord delivers him out of them all.

Psalm 34:4-19

He *heard* me and He *delivered* me from my fears. He changed my heart to fear His name. The word of God is powerful! By the fear of the Lord my life has changed, not by my own strength, but by His power. True transformation happened when I surrendered my will to His and I let Him do His work in my life. In complete surrender we speak His words that heal, enable, and empower us to be free. As a parent wants the best for his children, so much more God wants us to have the best of things in our lives. Nevertheless, fear is what the devil wants us to live with, always doubting, always afraid of what could go wrong.

I remember one day as I was driving back home, I felt like I couldn't breathe. I started having heart palpitations and I got very nauseous. When I got home, I told my husband that I wanted to go to the after-hours clinic at my doctor's office. When I got there, I realized that I was not going to see my regular doctor because it was late in the evening; I saw a nurse assistant that told me that all the symptoms I had were not a good sign and that I needed to go to the emergency room of the hospital and get a CT scan. This was not what I wanted to hear! I drove myself to the hospital in more panic. When I got there, I told the doctor in charge what I was told. I got the CT scan and they sent me home after injecting me with water saying that I was probably dehydrated. It was all a scheme from the devil and he was probably laughing at me.

The devil's job is to lie and to deceive and he works overtime to complete his job. He used fear to keep me from growing and trusting in the Lord. His main focus was to keep me down, sad, depressed, feeling like I was worth nothing. I couldn't do anything, everything was hard and unattainable and I was in that state of hopelessness and fear for a very long time. He attacks every area in our lives that we are most vulnerable to. He takes away every minute of peace we have. He plays with our emotions, our health, our finances and everything else that concerns us. He is awful and he is real.

I cannot count the times when thoughts of concern over things I had no control over came to my mind. Just when I thought I was walking in a straight line, fear paralyzed me and made me doubt. I realize that living by faith is no easy task. Walking by faith and not by sight is an everyday learning experience. Learning not to rely on the things that I can see and feel and just trusting in the Lord for His guidance and protection is what draws me closer to Him. It is in those moments that I can demonstrate my trust and confidence in Him, and then He shows Himself strong for me. He has never failed me, not once, not ever. The closer I draw to Him, the more I learn to trust Him.

"Fear of man will prove to be a snare, but whoever trusts in the Lord is kept safe" (Proverbs 29:25).

I realized that in my life I will come across two kinds of fear and I get to choose which fear I get to live with, because the fear of the Lord is made up of peace and joy, but the fear of man and other things involves worry and torment.

I have lived with fear as with a very close companion but I never realized that the worst fear and the one that offends God, is the fear of man. I was scared of people, of what they thought about me, of what they could do, not fully understanding that nothing happens unless God allows it to happen.

Have you ever been afraid of what other people thought about you? Have you ever done anything just to gain favor with them? Have you ever pretended to like someone just to be on their good side and because there was a certain interest behind it? I have done all of the above, and I can tell you from the bottom of my heart, it is no way to live.

My husband gave me one sermon after another regarding my fear of people. He detests it when I greet someone with a high voice, he says that it sounds fake and he often tells me, "Be yourself!" And the truth is, I always thought that I was being myself whenever I greeted them, but he saw in me what I failed to see: changing my voice changed the way I acted in front of them. All of a sudden, I became susceptible to let fear have dominion over me. My husband is bold and always says it like it is; he doesn't care to impress or look good in front of anyone. His fear has never been of others judging him. He puts his right foot forward and says what's in his heart, no matter who doesn't like it, and trusts God for the rest. Many times, I have desired to be like him.

The truth is, many of us change in front of people. We become something we are not with the desire to be liked, to be on their good side, or to impress them. Deep inside, we must admit that there is a fear of what they think about us. It took me a long time to understand that these are fears that God does not approve of. We are not here to please anyone but God. If God doesn't give us favor with people, I don't know what causes us to think that we will get it on our own.

In my pursuit for more information on the fear of man, I was led to read the fifteenth chapter of 1 Samuel.

I saw how God wants our obedience, our full obedience to His commandments. King Saul was rejected by God when he failed to carry out His commandment in complete obedience; he was rejected as king of Israel because of his fear of people (see 1 Samuel 15:24).

Abraham feared that the Egyptians might take away his life and he lied saying that Sarah was his sister. Because of his fear, he caused the Pharaoh to be struck with a plague (see Genesis 12). He also lied to Abimelech and almost caused him to die (see Genesis 20). These examples are warnings for us not to be consumed with the fear of man. It is not what man thinks or what man can do that matters, but what God says is what really matters.

The more I study God's word, the more I see His character. Living in the fear of Him becomes real when I see examples of the things that make Him angry. He is not pleased when we think we know better than Him. One of my favorite scriptures has always been, "Trust in the Lord with all your heart, and lean not to your own understanding; in all your ways acknowledge Him, and He shall direct your paths" (Proverbs 3:5-6).

There are things that I will never comprehend, yet I only have to trust and obey Him. I cannot try to make sense of the things I cannot or perhaps I will never understand. God's ways are not my ways. One thing I always talk myself into is obeying my husband. I don't always understand the way he opposes some of the decisions that I make concerning our household or regarding our daughter, but I remind myself to submit and obey because it's God's commandment. I have also learned to discern that many times, God might be testing me to see if I will obey my husband or let my will prevail. After all, this was an old pattern of mine.

God commanded Joshua, the successor of Moses, to be bold and courageous. Jesus said, "Don't be afraid, only believe." Scripture is filled with encouragement to fear not. The one fear worth having is the fear of God.

When we trust God, then we can act with such boldness as the three Hebrew young men did when king Nebuchadnezzar gave an order to bow down and worship the image of gold he set up. They refused to bow down being fully aware that their disobedience could cause them to die. When it was reported to the king that they disobeyed his orders, they were given a second chance to obey and bow down and worship the image. Otherwise, they were advised that they would be thrown immediately into the midst of a burning fiery furnace. They answered the king with confidence and boldness because they knew who their God was,

> *O Nebuchadnezzar, we have no need to answer you in this matter. If that is the case, our God whom we serve is able to deliver us from the burning fiery furnace, and He will deliver us from your hand, O king. But if not, let it be known to you, O king, that we do not serve your gods, nor will we worship the gold image which you have set up.*
>
> *Daniel 3:16-18*

God not only delivered them from the flames, but even the smell of fire was not on them. Can you imagine the reaction of all those who saw them walk out of the fire unharmed? Not only was God in the fire with them, but what was meant to cause them harm became a reason for their promotion.

I called myself a Christian for many years before I became aware of all this wisdom that the Lord manifested in my life. I still cannot believe how long I have lived without knowing or understanding that God is in control of all things. I tried very hard to fix things, obtain things, and work things out that just won't happen unless God wills it. I lived with stress, fear, and worry for things that were out of my control.

As I began to reach out to God for my every need, I knew that He was teaching me the things I needed to know to walk in the fear of Him and not of people or of other things. Life is never the same when you start seeking the Lord with the desire to know Him and when He starts giving you wisdom. He is an awesome God!

For the Lord gives wisdom; from his mouth come knowledge and understanding.

Proverbs 2:6 (NIV)

5

Higher Intervention

The fear of the Lord leads to life. (Proverbs 19:23 NIV)

One day, going through my husband's emails, I came across a note from his coworker in which she asked him to take her out for lunch so they can discuss his career at her company. This caught my attention very quickly because I was not going through his emails without his knowledge—he had his email address on my phone and he even asked me to check it from time to time. I knew that if he had anything to hide, he wouldn't be so casual about his privacy.

He had been searching for a job for a very long time without success of finding one. The same job that he got in a moment of desperation and need when we moved to Connecticut became his permanent job for years to come. I had recently quit my job in NYC in the beginning of the year and money was tight, but God was providing all along as we were learning to depend on Him.

He mentioned that his coworker offered to help him get a job in the company where she had a full-time job. I never paid too much attention to the matter—I knew that he was doing his best in his search for another job. He was surrounded by women at work and I have never been the jealous type, so I didn't think much of it. What caught my attention was her audacity to turn it into something else.

She not only said that she wanted to be taken out to eat, but she wanted him to give her a necklace that my husband had won as a prize which was meant to be for my daughter. In her note she asked, "Where is my necklace?" She referred to it as if it was already hers. I got irritated because she was trying to take advantage of my husband's need, and her flirtatious way in which she expressed herself, knowing that he was a married man, bothered me.

I confronted my husband about the note and I told him that I rather be poor and eat bread and water than allow him to entertain such a woman who obviously had the wrong intentions. I went on to say that she was not the owner of the company she worked for; therefore, she did not have a say in the matter. And even if she was the president of her company, she did not have the power to decide who gets a job, because only God determines our destiny.

This was my breaking point. My husband had been trying to get another job for the longest time, we were barely getting by, our relationship had not been good for years, and if that wasn't enough, his coworker wanted to be entertained by him. I felt like this was an attack on my marriage and I was not going to allow it! I had to get a higher intervention. We had been through years of hardship, miscommunication, and defeat. It was time to let God take charge of things and seek Him like never before.

This situation drove me to my knees and I cried out to God like I hadn't done it yet. I knew that I couldn't fight this battle on my own. I had to let God fight for us. My husband had tried to get another job on his own, but it was obviously not working. We had to seek Him with all of our hearts and let Him fix our lives, our finances, and our marriage. It took humility and submission to let go and let God, but this was our turning point.

Whatever gave my husband's coworker the idea that she could get in the middle of us, I don't know. Actually, I do know. The devil was looking for every opportunity to destroy me and destroy our marriage. He wanted me to yield to him in any way, and he was using anything and anyone to get to me. He probably thought that I would push my husband into the arms of another woman in desperation for a job. But the Lord was with me and I was about to let her and the whole world know, that we serve an Almighty God who is able to do exceedingly, abundantly, above all we can think or ask.

Within weeks of this incident, we saw God manifesting in our lives. We started praying as a family and we got closer to each other because our main focus was to get closer to Him. Our marriage became better and stronger, with less arguments and more communication. My husband kept on working with a different, more positive attitude. He was waiting on God to move in our lives.

One day at work, he met a new client who was a believer and he mentioned to her his desire to have another job. She gave him her business card and asked him to call her. The following week he went to get the job that he didn't seek or sold himself for because the Lord knows those who trust in Him.

"For the eyes of the Lord run to and from throughout the whole earth, to show Himself strong on behalf of those whose heart is loyal to Him" (2 Chronicles 16:9).

This was the first time I saw God work so closely and almost immediately after my prayers. This was eye opening for me and also for my husband. We knew without the shadow of a doubt that this job was of the Lord, what we were experiencing was in fact the work of God in our lives. God opened a position for my husband and He taught us that if we seek Him, He will work in our lives. We did not seek the favor of man alone; in prayer, we asked the Owner of all that is in the universe to get him a job. We saw the results of our prayers and we gave glory to God. He opened a door for my husband to have a good job.

The Lord saw that I was not willing to sell myself short for anything, and that my worry about the lack of resources was getting smaller because He was getting bigger in my life. I did not worry about my husband getting a job, and I was no longer thinking how we were going to survive and how much money we needed. I valued our marriage and my husband more than money. He saw that I did not want to allow the devil to come into our lives and destroy our family, I was willing to fight for what we had. I acknowledged that God was in control of everything and I started to let go of my worries and my fears by surrendering all my cares to Him.

Waiting on God and not losing heart is one of the most important things we can do when things seem to be going in the wrong direction. It is vital to step aside and let Him do His work in our lives. We often get in the way when we are trying to help Him as if we can do a better job. I don't think we realize the magnitude of His power and just the fact that He is God. He will not share His glory with anyone. When He works in our lives, it is crystal clear that He's done it all by Himself.

When God becomes bigger in our lives, everything else becomes smaller. When we let God work for us, we see change, we see increase, we see deliverance and healing. We don't have to live like the rest of the world when we have God on our side. We don't have to seek anyone's favor when the King of kings and Lord of lords is with us. We don't have to humble ourselves to anyone because the only One who is able to move our mountains is Him. Yes, we are to be humble, but not in submission to fear. Most importantly, we need to pray for Him to work. Prayer is what moves mountains.

"If God is for us, who can be against us?" (Romans 8:31)

In all this, I have learned that change comes with true and complete trust in the Lord. This experience was the beginning of a new phase in our lives. After years of bitterness, anger, and lack, transformation was starting to take place in our lives. I became humbler, spending longer periods of time in the presence of God. I wanted to see more of His work in our lives. I wanted to see change, I wanted peace instead of worry for the things that God knows that we need. I wanted the abundant life that Jesus promised to those who believe in Him. I wanted to know Him.

I was seeking the hand of God in our lives, but He was more interested in our hearts. Change was about to take place—slowly but surely—but it would take lots of prayer, patience, and time. I learned that God works one day at a time. He could have created heaven and earth in one day, or in a second if He wanted to, but He decided to do it one day at a time, and I saw the same pattern in our lives. I had to learn to wait on the Lord and let Him do His work in His time and in His will.

Whatever you are facing today, know that you can pray your care to Him who is able to move every barrier of impossibility. He is never closer than when you find yourself in your deepest need. His word says that all things are possible for the one who believes.

> *He holds success in store for the upright, he is a shield to those whose walk is blameless, for he guards the course of the just and protects the way of his faithful ones.*
>
> *Proverbs 2:7-8 (NIV)*

SHIRLEY HERNANDEZ

6

Understanding God's Love

"See what great love the Father has lavished on us, that we should be called children of God! And that is what we are!"
(1 John 3:1 NIV)

    I went through the worst stage of postpartum depression right after I had my daughter and it lasted a couple of years. I remember going to the doctor and telling him how I felt and all I got from him was a prescription for anti-depressants. He only did his job by doing what he knew would help me feel better. Deep inside my heart, I was longing for God's help. In those moments, of deep sadness and uncertainty, I desired His presence more than anything in the world. So, I never took anything, but that was my own decision. Perhaps taking medication would've helped me feel better sooner, but I wanted more than just to feel better, I wanted to be set free from oppression and from fears.

I knew that only God was able to do that for me. So, I decided to seek the Lord instead. I didn't know what else to do. No one I knew had gone through what I was going through, so how could they have understood the way I felt? There was pain, and fear, and desperation. I had many sleepless nights when all I wanted to do was cry myself to sleep. I wanted to feel better, I did not want to go through life sad and negative, and I wanted my joy back or rather, I wanted to know what true joy was. My heart was longing for the peace of God which is only found in Him. Only He understood what I was going through. Only He knew it all and He was there for me all along.

In the midst of my depression and fears, during the times that my husband and I used to fight, and when I felt like the whole world was against me, I found God's love. The moments that I felt the worst and most hopeless are the times I have felt God's most amazing love. I have sensed His presence, I have seen His works, and His mercy and His grace. He's never let me down. Even when I didn't know Him, I drew my strength from Him. His promises kept me going from day to day. I did not lose heart because I knew that He was there walking with me.

Journal notes:

For the last couple of months, there's been a deep desire to know God and to have a relationship with Him. He is my Father and my Creator and my Healer, of course I want to know Him.

*****

Lord, I am far away from being perfect, but I'm close enough to you to know that without you, I am nothing. You are my God and my life. I want to learn of you and from you every day. I know that there is so much that needs to change in me. Help me to be patient, to be kind, to be loving, to be good, to be faithful, to have self-control, to be gentle and to love more.

Today I have decided that I will learn to be closer to what you want me to be. Today, I will learn to put a zipper in my mouth and to watch every word that comes out of it. Help me not to say anything negative.

*****

Lord, I know you love me. You are patient. You are kind. Please help me to be like You. I want to be patient and kind at all times. Thank you for loving me enough to help me see where I need to grow. I trust You!

The Lord has been teaching me about understanding that the only thoughts He has for me are good, for a good future... positive, hopeful thoughts. He wants me to understand that unless I believe in my heart that this is true and real, it will be hard to receive all the blessings that are meant for me.

*****

"For my soul trusts in you and in the shadow of your wings, I will make my refuge. Whenever I am afraid, I will trust in you. In God I have put my trust. I will not fear. What can flesh do to me? Cast your burden on the Lord and He shall sustain you, He shall never permit the righteous to be moved." (Psalm 57:1, 56:3,4, 55:22)

Thank you, Lord. You are my refuge, you are my strength. Every word that comes out of your mouth feeds my spirit and my soul. You are faithful and I thank you for always being on my side. Blessed be your holy name!

*****

A couple of weeks ago, I sought the Lord in a moment of desperation. I called out for mercy with this in mind, "I know you love me." He heard my prayer and He healed me. In the days to come, I saw how He worked in my life. One day at a time, He showed me how my attitude needed to change. He gave me wisdom and understanding by His word and He set me free from my affliction. I used His word as a weapon to fight the lies of the enemy, because I know that God loves me and He showed me His love over and over again. He did not turn His face from me in my distress, but He opened His arms and said, "Do not fear." God is faithful and merciful. He longs for us to seek His face and in His presence, there is fulness of joy. He then showed me Psalms 16-17, and, 18:

We put our confidence in Him. Psalm 16
We pray for His protection. Psalm 17

We are delivered from evil. Psalm 18
Thank you, Lord!

In my walk with God, I had to come to understand that His love for me is infinite. I am not the owner of me. I was born with a purpose and He planned out my destiny even before I was born. When God takes a hold of you, He won't let go. He is patient and kind. He is there to lift you up when you hit rock bottom, not to tell you, "I told you so," but to tell you, "Do not fear, I love you, I won't let you go."

When you feel depressed as I was, when others tell you "I never went through it, it never happened to me," God is there to let us know that He knows exactly how we feel, and that He cares because He bore our pain in His own flesh and blood. How can you refuse this kind of love? How can you walk away from your Father and Creator who loves you regardless of your fears and your mistakes? You simply can't! This is a love that only God Himself offers you. It is a love that is beyond comprehension of which the apostle Paul spoke about in Romans:

> *Who shall separate us from the love of Christ? Shall tribulation, or distress, or persecution, or famine, or nakedness, or peril, or a sword?... For*

> *I am persuaded that neither death nor life, nor angels nor principalities nor powers, nor things present nor things to come, nor height nor depth, nor any other created thing, shall be able to separate us from the love of God which is in Christ Jesus our Lord.*
>
> Romans 8:35, 38-39

I know that God loves me. Not because I think I'm good, because I'm not—no one is (see Mark 10:18). Not because I think I'm special, not because I call myself a Christian, not because I read my Bible, but because of Jesus' sacrifice on the cross. He died so that we might be in right standing with our heavenly Father and have a unique, close relationship with Him. Jesus' death on the cross was the ultimate gift to the world to demonstrate God's love for us. God's love is eternal. He loved us and continues to love us and He will still love us forever because that is who He is, Love.

It took me a very long time to understand that every time I make a mistake, every time I fail to believe that He has good plans for me, He is not angry or surprised as if He didn't know that I was going to fail Him. In His infinite mercy, He knew it all before any of my days on earth began. He is not caught by surprise every time I act in disbelief or in fear, He is not mad at me because

He loves me. The devil is a liar and a deceiver and he wants me to feel guilty and bad about the very thing I already asked God to forgive me for.

Every time I am tested by the Lord and I fail, it is not so I can get disappointed, it is for me to understand what is in my heart. Because He loves me, He gives me the wisdom to know what is inside my heart that is preventing me from growing and bearing good fruit. God is good and faithful. Every test, every trial, and every temptation of the devil should only lead me to grow more in the knowledge of Him.

> *Remember how the Lord God led you all the way in the wilderness these forty years, to humble and test you in order to know what was in your heart, whether or not you would keep his commands.*
> *Deuteronomy 8:2 (NIV)*

God wants me to know that He loves me. He knows that there will be stepping stones in my growth. I cannot think in any way that He is angry and ready to punish me for every mistake I make. He wants me to respect Him, love Him, and obey Him as my Father and my God. But He wants me to seek Him and pray to Him with the faith of a child, believing that I will be heard and I will receive everything I ask according to His will.

I am completely convinced of God's love for me. God loves me and He loves you. Are you convinced of His love for you? Believe it. Receive it. Cherish it. Nurture it. Hide it in your heart and pray that you might be filled with complete assurance of His love for you every day of your life, because He loved you, He loves you, and He will never stop loving you.

> *And I pray that you, being rooted and firmly established in love, may be able to comprehend with all the saints what is the length and width, height and depth of God's love, and to know the Messiah's love that surpasses knowledge, so you may be filled with all the fullness of God.*
>
> *Ephesians 3:17-19 (HCSB)*

Time in His Presence is an Investment of High Return

"Lord, you are the God who saves me; day and night I cry out to You. May my prayer come before You; turn Your ear to my cry." (Psalm 88:1-2 NIV)

One cold Saturday morning, my husband went to work very early. He left the house while my daughter and I were still sleeping. I always had the habit of turning off my cell phone the night before until I woke up the next morning. That particular morning, we slept in late and when I turned on my phone, I saw that there were several messages from my husband saying that the car was trapped in the snow.

I rushed to call him and he explained that he had taken the side road to work, a road that had no traffic at all. He urged me to rush and bring him a shovel to try and get him out. We quickly got dressed and rushed out of the house with a shovel and gloves. When we arrived, my husband had been trying to dig the car out for the last two hours with no success at all. In desperation, I started praying and hoping that the shovel would help him, but there was no significant progress.

It was cold and icy, woods on both sides of the road and no traffic at all, but I kept on praying. Soon after, I saw a car pull up and a couple came out to help him dig around the car without any success. A few minutes later, a white van pulled over and a man started talking to the couple, they seemed to be friends. I was sitting inside the car with my daughter watching how these perfect strangers were trying so hard to get my husband's car out of the snow. Then, all of a sudden, they told my husband to get in the car, start it, and the man in the white van started pushing the car out little by little until it finally came out.

As I started thanking God in relief, I saw the man with the van walking towards my car, I rolled down my window and I said, "Thank you so much, I had been praying for things to work out," he looked at me straight in my eyes and very firmly said, "Don't ever underestimate the power of God!" He turned around and left. Were they angels that God sent to help us? I always believed that they were. I will never forget the way the man with the white van spoke to me. The look in his eyes and the way he spoke to me led me to believe that he was sent from God indeed.

"For He will command His angels concerning you to guard you in all your ways" (Psalm 91:11).

There are angels all around us and they are ready to be dispatched by God at any time we call out for help, but we have to pray and let Him know that we need Him. God wants our dependence and He wants to help us in every way.

Journal notes:
Thank you, Lord, you've done it again. You are faithful! My daughter has had the desire to have a puppy for a while now, and we started praying for one lately since we all would like a dog. A couple of days ago, I looked at a folder we have had for two years now and it has pictures of puppies. I recall saying in my heart and then to my daughter, "We want a puppy just like this one in the picture." Yesterday, we got a call and an email from a breeder with pictures of the same puppy we saw in the folder— same breed, same color!

Lord, you are an awesome God, you are an amazing Father and, in your presence, there is fullness of everything! I want to thank you for loving us. I want to thank you for providing for us, for the countless blessings we receive from you every day. Thank you for all the benefits of serving you, you are an awesome Father!

"Take delight in the Lord, and he will give you the desires of your heart" (Psalm 37:4 NRSV).

Those were the days that my eight-year-old daughter wanted to get a puppy. She was fixed on the idea that her daddy would get her one and she would not take no for an answer. My husband contacted his former co-worker who used to breed puppies and she referred us to another breeder. When we got the email with the pictures of the puppies she had available, I knew that the Lord had heard our prayers. Those were the puppies from the folder that we had pointed out.

The fact that we got the same puppy we asked for was no coincidence, but the work of God alone. His word says that if we delight ourselves in the Lord, He will give us the desires of our heart. We sure got the desire of our hearts! We not only got the perfect puppy, but the perfect addition to our family.

When my daughter asks her daddy for anything, his desire is to get for her whatever she asks him for. He wants to give to her the desires of her heart because he wants to make her happy. How much more must our

Father in Heaven desire to give us the things that we ask for? I don't have to be concerned about anything in this life because the Lord is faithful and true, and if there is something that I desire to have and it's in His will for me to have it, He will give it to me. He knows my needs and my desires even before I ask for anything.

Years ago, as I was in a public place, I looked down on my boots and I saw that they were worn out and old, and in my heart, I said, "I need another pair of boots." Now, I did not mention it to anyone, only God knew what I desired in my heart. Just a few weeks later one day when I came back home, my husband had a box that he wanted me to open before Christmas. When I opened the box and saw a pair perfect brown boots, I knew that the Lord had answered the desire that I had in my heart.

My husband never bought shoes or boots for me! He always let me pick out what I wanted to wear and he never got involved in it. I never mentioned to him that I wanted or needed a pair of boots, and I did not want to ask for it anyway. We were living on one income and I did not feel comfortable asking for something new if there were other more important things that we needed to have. After I opened the box, I shared with my husband of my desire to have those perfect boots that he had gotten for me and how the Lord provided. I thanked the Lord for His goodness, it was He who provided the boots and it was He who let my husband know of my desire and there was no doubt in my heart.

Another time, when I was just starting to trust in the Lord for provision and when I thought we couldn't afford to get the many things I desired, as I was making my bed every morning, I kept telling myself, "We need new pillows." The following week, my mother-in-law called me and told me that she had purchased some pillows that she really liked and that she wanted to get the same pillows for us. Days later, I had all brand-new pillows.

Just weeks later when my parents came to visit, my mother pulled out of her bag an entire set of facial moisturizers and makeup. When I saw it all, I sobbed while I told her and my daughter that God had provided the very thing that I was hoping to get. I also told them the story about the pillows and how God supplied the desires of my heart.

I could go on and on talking about the provision of God in our lives. Little and big things, it all comes from Him. He makes all things happen in our lives. When you start walking in the fear of the Lord, you don't just look at the natural, but little things that seem insignificant become the supernatural. Living by faith is trusting in Him to provide all things in every way.

These experiences of the puppy, the boots, and many more are the gestures of a God who is concerned about my every need in this life. I know that there is nothing that I desire that the Lord will not give me if my desire is to do His will and to serve Him. I love the way God works, when He does something, no one can take the credit for it because He does it in ways that you know it's only Him and no one else. Thank you, Jesus!

"I called to the Lord in my distress...and my cry to Him reached His ears" (Psalm 18:6 HCSB).

Years ago, I fell and broke my wrist. I still remember that day as if it was yesterday. I remember that I never felt such pain in my life. When I got to the emergency room and was waiting for a doctor to see me, I prayed for God to take away the pain and to make me feel better. He heard me and healed me. Not only did He heal my broken bones, but He also healed my broken spirit. I had been gloomy and complaining a lot during those days. He revived me and made me whole, completely whole. The word of God is medicine to my body and health to my bones. This is not just a belief, it is founded solely on scripture (see Proverbs 3:8). God's word healed me and made me strong in moments of pain and great fear.

Journal notes,

Three days ago, I fell and broke my wrist. Oh, how painful! Lord, I know You are with me, I just know You are! You are my healer and by Your stripes I am healed. This too, will work out for good in my life, maybe I don't see it now or how, but I know it will. Help me to keep a good attitude and to have a hopeful heart.

*****

Days before my fall, one night I clearly heard in my spirit, "Things will start to get bad, pray." I believe that it was the spirit of God warning me that this would happen. Today I read the book of Job and I know that my redeemer lives. I don't like this, it is painful, it is uncomfortable, it is frustrating, but I know that my God whom I serve is still on the throne and He is in control of all things. Today more than ever, I understand that nothing happens without God letting it happen, and this too shall pass and my God will get all the glory.

*****

I know you love me, Lord. I will fear not because you are still on the throne.
I might be hard pressed on every side, yet not crushed.
Perplexed, but not in despair.
Persecuted, but not forsaken.
Struck down, but not destroyed.
I will not lose heart; my light affliction is only for a moment...

*****

Here I am, Lord, two weeks and two days from my fall. Today I went to see another orthopedic doctor. After going through all the pain last week, I still know that You are God and you are in control of all things. Nothing is a surprise to You. If this happened to polish the rough edges out of me, so be it, let your work be done in my life. I do not question what You allow to happen in my life. I want to grow up and become all you want me to be. I know your thoughts are higher than my thoughts, and I also know you love me.

This period of my life was very painful. I never broke a bone in my life. Seeing the odd shape of my broken wrist scared me. I went through a lot of pain because I was even scared to take pain medication, but my comfort in my affliction was that God was with me; even the pain was relieved by His presence. This knowledge was what kept me going strong and confident. I often wrote self-assuring words, I claimed His promises for my life, I spoke His word out loud, and all along I knew that I was going to learn something out of it all, and I did.

I learned that if God allows something to happen in my life there is a bigger purpose in it. I may not understand it all but I have to trust that He knows best and that He loves me and has good plans for me. I learned that God doesn't leave me alone in the middle of a storm. He is always present because He is in control of all things and nothing catches Him by surprise. He wants me to take hold of His strength. He wants me to be strong in Him and to know that all things work together for good to those who love God, to those who are called according to His purpose. (Romans 8:28)

Because of my fall, I got even closer to my daughter. She became my other hand as she helped me with the things I could not do alone in the house. She also wanted me closer to her and months later, she wanted me to wait for her inside her ballet school. While she danced and I started writing in the perfect setting, with beautiful classical music in the background, I was inspired to write whatever came to my mind. I did not know then that the things that God was leading me to write about, just months later, were going to be written in this book. God leads us in ways we can't even imagine. He is an awesome God!

Prayer changed my life for the better and I can't even begin to tell you the peace and the joy it has brought into my life. I don't have to understand how God works in my life, I just have to trust Him and surrender it all to Him. Is it easy? No, but what choice do I have? God is in charge of all things not me, and I don't have to do life alone when He is near. I don't have to depend on someone to hear me when I feel anxious or when things are not going my way. I can come before the throne of Him who is able to lift every burden and every distress in my life, and turn every tear into joy for this is what He does best.

I cannot forget that prayer is what got me through my toughest moments in time. I cannot forget that without prayer I would not have the peace and the joy that He allows me to enjoy today, because I was not always this way. I cannot forget that years ago, I used to worry about everything and today those things that used to steal my peace and joy, have little or no power over me. The closer I get to Him, the more I know Him, the more I see the pattern of how He works in my life and the lives of others. God wants this closeness with us. He desires it more than we do.

"Be still and know that I am God" (Psalm 46:10).

Time with God is the most important thing that I can do for myself and for my family. We live in such a busy world that requires that we multitask and it is hard to find enough time to sit quietly, meditate on God's word, and pray. It has been a learning process for me to sit in the Lord's presence, but I have learned to discipline myself to find time for God because He has been my shield and my strength.

I have learned to depend on the Lord for health, peace, finances, leading, joy, and everything else. So how is it that sometimes a day goes by and I seem to be too busy to spend time with Him? Those are the days when I put more effort into things I'm working on and nothing works out right. When I give the Lord first place in my life, first thing in the morning, then everything else falls into place. I have tested this concept several times, and time and time again this proves that the word of God is true and it never fails. When I make prayer and meditation my priority, He blesses my day, increases my productivity and He puts joy and peace into my heart. Somehow the day has enough hours to do everything I need to do, and I have time left over to actually enjoy time with my family and do the things we like.

On the other hand, when I rush in the morning and throughout the day without spending much time with the Lord, I become weary, irritable, and glum. Those are the times that I know I need more of Jesus in me. Hanging out with Jesus makes me want to be more like Him and I end up being a better mother and a better wife.

Two things motivate me to wake up early in the morning to spend time with the Lord. I see it as my investment and His return. One is the fear of Him and the other is the benefits of spending time in His presence. The fear of Him keeps me aware that without Him I can do nothing; therefore, I long to be empowered by His presence in my life. The benefits of spending time with God are priceless. My wisdom comes from Him, my hope, my faith, my health, my joy, my strength, everything I need and want is found only in Him. This knowledge is what drives me to know Him more and more every single day. The more I seek Him, the more I know Him.

My days are better when I put Him first in my schedule, it is the best time to seek Him and say,

Good morning, Lord. Thank you for this new, wonderful day that you have made. Thank you for one more day in our lives. Thank you for loving us and keeping us. Thank you that we are whole and healthy. Thank you for a cozy house, food to eat, clothes to wear and the countless blessings You provide for us every day.

Thank you for your word which leads me and guides me. Thank you for all the things that I have and even for what I don't have, because you know better than to let me have that which I am not ready to have. Thank you for all the blessings I will receive this day.

When I start my morning this way, I am positioning myself to receive all the blessings that God has prepared for me to have. I can be confident that no matter what happens during the day, He is with me. Much of the wisdom for the day and my daily bread was given to me first thing in the morning. I have recorded the many times that He gave me a scripture in the morning, and later in the day I realized that, had I paid more attention to it, I would've had more insight to deal with whatever came up during my day.

How about the times that I woke up with a thought in my mind to guide me and teach me? It was all Him! The name of this book was given to me first thing in the morning, while it was still dark. I woke up one day and I wrote it down. Pray Your Care. It was a gift of God. In all humility I can tell you that I did not have to search for it. I let Him lead me and guide me and He has. He is our wisdom and understanding and it is free of charge for whoever will receive it. That is the power of God!

When I pray, I acknowledge that He is God and that I am at His mercy. I thank Him for my life and for the life of those around me and for everything else. He owns it all and in His perfect goodness He lets us enjoy it all. I know that God wants me to spend time with Him and my desire to do His will draws me closer to Him. If anything will be accomplished in my life, will be the result of my obedience to Him. The longer I live, the more I realize that life is only worth living in His presence.

Prayer is the most amazing tool that God has given us. Because of Jesus, prayer is the privilege to come before the Father's throne of grace with the certainty that we will be heard and answered. Meditating on His word, seeking His face every day, and acknowledging that He is in control of all things is something I desire to do every day because by it, I am set free. I lay my burdens before Him and in return He gives me His peace.

We are the product of the environment we live in, the people we hang out with, and the choices that we make. Whatever is going on around us affects the way we live and the way we act. I know better than to think that anything good will come out of me if I don't seek Him. The more time I spend with Him the more I become like Him. Every day we become more like the one we are spending time with, and the character of Jesus is what draws me near to Him. We will live to please the world or to please God. We will live to honor Him or the world and our own desires. But we have one life and if we are going to live it well and have God's peace, we have to pray.

When Jesus went to pray right before He got arrested, He asked His disciples to stay awake and pray and three times He found them sleeping. Did you ever ask yourself what was He trying to teach us in all this? What did He want us to learn? He was in a moment of deep distress. His arrest was at hand. He was about to go through the biggest trial of His life, yet in his last moments with them, He not only asked them to pray, but He was praying for them and for all of us, as recorded in the book of John 17.

If Jesus prayed being the Son of God, I realize how much more we should pray. Our spirit is willing to pray, to read the scriptures, to have a relationship with the Lord. We long to do all these things, but what happens when it really comes down to it? Time is a factor and somehow, we always seem to be too busy to do the things that honor God and give Him glory, we neglect our prayer life, and before we know it, we find ourselves exhausted, stressed, and in despair, running back to the arms of God and crying out for help. It seems to me like if He just lets us have our own way because He knows that sooner or later, when we come face-to-face with our challenges and the things we cannot fix on our own, we will run back to Him. It happens to all of us. It's a circle that goes around and comes back to the starting point.

I can't count the times when the fear of what I cannot control wants to rule over my thoughts, but remembering Jesus' words to pray, ask, seek, knock, believe, and not fear, I fight my fears with the strength of Him who is with me. Scripture is full of encouragement to seek the Lord's face in prayer for wisdom and to pray without ceasing for everything, in everything, and at all times. When I pray and my burdens become lighter, I am able to have peace in the midst of my conflicts. I pray and my vision becomes clear and I am able to see the light at the end of the tunnel. Just when I thought there was no hope, the light shines on my way out of the darkness. Prayer is a constant reminder for me not to give up.

In my walk with the Lord, I learned that scripture is a weapon which Jesus used when He was tempted by the devil, and I learned to use it in my own struggles. If He had the scriptures in His heart and mind to defeat Satan so that he would flee, I need to arm myself with His word and speak it out loud. The word of God is our defense and our weapon in the spiritual world.

Let's live by example. Let's be committed to doing everything that Jesus commanded so that we might live an abundant life. He came that we might live, and live more abundantly in every aspect of our lives. If we truly believe that we have a manual for success in the Bible, why not apply His teaching to our lives especially when it comes to prayer. The word of the Lord is light, it is proven and it is truth. Let's build our house on the Rock and watch as storms come and go while we stand strong, fully able to withstand whatever comes our way because we know who holds us in the palm of His hand.

Today as you read and meditate on the word of God, my prayer for you is that you find a few moments to seek the Lord in prayer. He is our Father and our God and He longs to have a relationship with us and to answer our prayers. You don't need to go to church, He is right there where you are. He longs to hear your prayer because He wants to bless you.

Don't rob yourself of a blessing and neglect to seek His face today. Prayer is talking to God, thanking him for his goodness in our lives, and yes, even requesting whatever needs we have. God begins to work in our lives when we seek Him in prayer. I encourage you to never let a day go by without finding some time to spend on the one thing that really matters, your relationship with the Lord. Remember that our lives and the length of our days are found in Him (see Deuteronomy 30:20).

> *Anything you ask the Father in My name, He will give you…Ask and you will receive, so that your joy may be complete.*
>
> John 16:23-24

Motherhood is a Gift from God

"If you, then, though, you are evil, know how to give good gifts to your children, how much more will your Father in heaven give good things to those who ask Him!" (Matthew 7:11 NIV)

Journal notes:
Recently, I have been asking the Lord to help me be a good mother. This afternoon, as I was cleaning, I found a card in which I had written some scriptures for memorization on how the Lord directs our steps. As I was washing dishes, I decided to memorize them. Later in the afternoon, we went to get a cupcake for my daughter along with some other things that we wanted to buy for her, today is her birthday. We came home just in time to get ready quickly and go to ballet.

As I was grabbing my bag, I realized that I did not have my wallet in it and I panicked. Not the right thing to do for me, I have been working on not panicking about anything but clearly, I still need work. I started looking for my wallet and *the first thing that came into my mind is that I left it in the last store we went to. My husband told me to call the store, but he also reminded me that I take time too lightly, and it was getting late for my daughter's class. I let everything he said stress me for a moment and then I remembered that I had seen my wallet last in the car. As I walked out to get into the car, I saw it in the floor of the garage, it probably fell when I got off the car.*

As I was driving my daughter to ballet, she said that I yelled at her when I told her that I did not want her wallet. She had offered me to give me her wallet when I was looking for mine, I didn't even notice the kind gesture she had when I was in the middle of my panic moment. I apologized and I said that I was never going to react the way I did any more and she said, "Be careful what you promise." When she said that, I realized that I was vowing something that I had to keep no matter what.

When I came back home, I went straight to pray because I don't know what else to do. I did not want to make my daughter feel bad, especially today, it is her birthday today. I read a couple of scriptures and then I heard clearly in my spirit, "You are asking Me to help you to be a good mother, how will you become one if you cannot see your mistakes. Trust in Me and watch Me work in you."

I never noticed that my beautiful daughter innocently offered me to give me her wallet to replace mine, she later told me that she thought I needed money. This act of kindness and surrender of something that belonged to her touched my heart. The reason I wanted my wallet was because I had my driver's license and other documentation in it, but perhaps the real reason I wanted my wallet was because I was terrified at the thought of losing it. I failed to look at my daughter's generous behavior because I was caught up in in a moment of fear. At the end of the day was it going to matter if I lost it? Anything is replaceable, but once again I let fear take control over me.

The Lord is working in me and I cannot question His work; all I have to do is surrender my will and my emotions to Him. I don't understand everything that happens or why it happens, but I know that the same God who loves me enough to help me see my mistakes will also help me to be a good mother. I don't want to miss my moment because of things that don't matter. I don't want my daughter to grow up with the feeling that material things are more important to me than she is. I don't want to live to regret anything, especially when it comes to my daughter. God has entrusted me with her life to care for and I want to do it to the best of my ability. She needs to know that she is loved not just with words, but with actions that show how valuable she is. She needs to know that I am here for her and that I care about all the things that are significant to her.

As a mother, it is my calling and my responsibility to give her direction in her life. It is my job to pray for her, to encourage her, to lift up her spirit, to inculcate morality, wisdom and knowledge in her heart. There are things that our children ought to learn at home like respect and values if we don't want them to mimic what they see in the world. One of my favorite scriptures in raising her has been, "Train up a child in the way he should go, and when he is old he will not depart from it" (Proverbs 22:6).

God has given me the privilege and the wisdom to homeschool my daughter, and I learned to take my assignment very seriously. Bible reading has become a must before we do any school work. If I teach my daughter everything, but I fail to teach her to seek and know God, then my work is in vain. I am convinced that the most important thing I can do for her is to teach her to seek the Lord and to meditate on His promises. "Now this is eternal life: that they may know You, the only true God, and Jesus Christ, whom You have sent" (John 17:3 NIV).

As I watch my daughter grow up, I realize that she will need me to grow up spiritually with her. I cannot remain at the same spiritual level that I was even a year ago. When she was little, I was feeding her physically and caring for her in all the ways she could not care for herself. As she gets older, her spirit needs to be fed as well and that is where I come in.

The most important thing that I can do right at this moment is to be the kind of mother that God wants me to be. If I want my daughter to serve God and become a great woman of faith, then I must become one first. As my husband says, she needs to learn by example. I need to model the kind of relationship that she will have with the Lord one day and I need to live out my faith in front of her. I cannot teach her something that I am not practicing myself. She will learn to do and say the same things she sees me do and say. Her attitudes will be in line with the attitudes that I display. Nothing gives me the right to correct her if my behavior is opposite to what I am teaching her. It becomes a contradiction and I noticed that she is listening and observing everything I say and do.

Long ago, I met a woman who seemed to become very nervous with her son's disorder which made him hyperactive. When I spoke to her about prayer, she said that she would not talk about religion because she grew up with a mother whose behavior was different at home and at church. She was disappointed because she had seen her mother attend church religiously, but her behavior confused her leading her to believe that people who attend church are nothing but religious.

When I heard what she had to say I realized that as Christ followers, we need to live out our faith at church and at home alike. It becomes confusing for our children if we display a different attitude in church than the one we have at home. A while ago, I heard a story about a woman who wanted to impress her pastor when he paid her a visit in her house. She told her children to go and grab the book they read every day. Thinking that her children would bring the Bible to her, she was speechless when they brought a department store catalog instead. As funny as this story may sound, our children are observing our actions, listening to every word we say, and watching how we are spending our time.

I grew up with parents who used to fight all the time. There was no violence, but their words to each other pierced more than physical thumps. I remember that after every fighting episode, my mom would go inside the bathroom to smoke. My sister and I used to ask her not to, but she said it calmed her down. When I had my daughter, the smell of smoke used to bother me so much that I would get very angry when I saw someone smoking. My neighbor next door used to smoke every day right outside her house watching her kids play and I despised it. I never understood why it used to irritate me so much until I realized that it reminded me of my mother's ways of dealing with her problems.

Unfortunately, I was never close to my mother. I was afraid to tell her anything for fear of her reaction because she used to get upset over everything. In my lowest moments, I wish she would've been there for me, not to make me feel worse as she often did, but to encourage me and to let me know that she was there not matter what. I don't blame her for the way she was, only God knows why our relationship was not the way I wish it would've been. Maybe because of that reason, I made it my goal to give my daughter the confidence and the assurance that she can tell me anything by becoming her friend. I don't just want her to see me as her mother, but as a mentor and a friend in whom she can trust.

I see how my daughter observes me. I know that she is listening to everything that comes out of my mouth. I am constantly reminded by her to keep my word, to practice everything I teach her, and to be on time. It is as if through her, God Himself reminds me of the things that are important in raising her. I learned to listen and understand that there is a purpose and a meaning in everything. I've also learned that there is so much we can learn from our children. It's all in the details because the smallest gestures matter the most.

Some of us might think that the things we say and do are not affecting our children, but I know they are. Every word that comes out of our mouth has the potential to heal or to hurt, to encourage or to let down, to uplift or to bring low. Our actions are being weighed not only by God but by those closest to us. One day we will have to give an account to the Lord for every careless word that comes out of our mouth (see Matthew 12:36). Because of this fact, it leads me to watch the way I'm living, the things I'm saying, and my behavior. Our children are God's most precious gift to us and I know that we all desire to bless them.

I feel blessed that the Lord has given me the chance to become a mother and to know what it is like to love a child. Because of this amazing love that I have for my daughter, I can better understand God's love for me. I cannot comprehend a love greater and purer than the love for a child. It is a love that is not selfish, it is giving without expecting anything in return. It is a fearless love. It is loving without being afraid to love and without thinking whether or not your love will be reciprocated. It is a love that nourishes and builds up.

The fact is that this love that I feel for my daughter is the kind of love that God loves me with, and I know that this is an understatement, because His love is so much bigger and greater than anything I can fathom. The love of God gave us Jesus Christ so that we might live in harmony with the Father. I cannot picture a love greater than that.

I want to be the kind of mother that God wants me to be. Furthermore, I want to make sure that I am doing everything I possibly can to make sure that my daughter receives the love of God through me. I don't have to convince anyone that I am trying to be the best mother that I can be, I just have to be me and lean on the One who is able to work in and through me. Everything I need, I will find in Jesus.

Today, as you think about the children that God has given you to care for, as you look at your relationship with each and every one of them, take a moment to meditate on the job that God has given us to do. Let us come to the realization that God knew what we were going to be like even before He gave us any children. He is not surprised at the good or poor relationship we have with our children. He is not disappointed with our mistakes. He knew it all even before we became parents. We can only try to become better and as we do, let's consider the impact it will make for future generations. Let us become all that God has created us to be, let us become the kind of parents that pray for our children and for our children's children all to the honor and glory of God.

Lord, you know our hearts and minds. Nothing we say or do will ever be a surprise to you. Lead us to establish an example of goodness and fear of you in front of our children. Help us to lead our children on paths of righteousness and faith. Help us to raise a generation that will understand the meaning of the fear of the Lord. Help us to understand that the plans that you have for us are for good and not evil, to know that we have a future and a hope in You. Fill us with the knowledge of Your will and give us the courage and strength to obey your commandments and serve you. Thank you, Father. Amen.

> *Love the Lord your God with all your heart and with all your soul and with all your strength. These commandments that I give you today are to be on your hearts. Impress them on your children. Talk about them when you sit at home and when you walk along the road, when you lie down and when you get up.*
>
> *Deuteronomy 6:5-7 (NIV)*

A Command with a Promise

"Honor your father and mother," which is the first commandment with a promise: "so that it may go well with you and that you may enjoy long life on the earth"
(Ephesians 6:2-3 NIV).

Years ago, on one of my parent's first visits after retiring, I had a conversation with my mom which led me to speak about the goodness of God and of His power. I don't know if my relationship with the Lord caught her by surprise, but I was shocked by what she said to me. "I don't understand how someone can speak so much about God," she said. At the time I did not understand the meaning of her words, but later on I did.

I was speaking about God and I had a relationship with Him, but my actions and my attitudes were speaking louder about me. In other words, I was not practicing what I was preaching. I remember that on that particular summer, I had a huge argument with her. I disrespected her by answering back to every word she said to me, I made her feel bad, and I was even annoyed with her presence. I was not keeping the fifth commandment which says to honor you father and your mother (see Exodus 20:12).

The first thing that I wanted to do was to dig into the word and see what "Honor you father and your mother really meant." I read the Bible and I prayed for God to help me see what I needed to see. I wanted to find something in scripture that would justify my behavior, I did not want to accept God's commandment because in my eyes, I was right and she was wrong. Unfortunately for me, I was relying on my feelings and on my own understanding.

My mom and I have clashed since I can remember. My memory bank is filled with pictures of arguments, conflicts, and disagreements of all sorts, but I thank God for not allowing those memories of things past to poison my heart today as they did previously. I always thought that my mom had an evil heart. I judged her behavior and I criticized her. I took sides with my dad many times because I did not like the way she treated him. After my daughter was born, I was convinced that she was a despicable human being.

When I started going to church, I was complaining about my mom constantly because I was filled with bitterness toward life and toward her; I wanted to let it all out. I used to go to prayer services and kneel by the altar to sob like a baby because I was hurting. My anger towards her was causing me physical stress. *"Poor me,"* I thought. I was the victim of my circumstances. One day, God allowed me to leave "poor me" at the altar and get over my bitterness and anger, and get my courage and my strength from Him.

How easy it is to judge those closest to us without realizing that their behavior might be a consequence of what they have been through in life. It is easy to say, "I would never do that, or I would never say such a thing." I have. I told myself not once, but many times, "I never want to be like my mother," because I disliked her and everything about her. Not even for a moment did I pause to think about her life and what led her to behave the way she did. I never saw that behind her anger and rage was a frightened, wounded soul who did not want to let go of the arrows that pierced her heart.

In the past couple of years, God opened my eyes to see my mother's pain which she has lived with most of her life. Her arguments with my dad brought out the worst in her; since I can remember, their relationship to each other has always been hanging by a thread. My mom was focused on bringing back a past that deeply hurt her, and my dad wanted to bury it. Her pain turned into bitterness and her unforgiveness into rage and fear.

I often hear that hurting people hurt other people; this could not be more precise when it comes to my mother. Out of her own pain she hurt us. But I know that deep inside her bleeding heart, there is a seed of love for us.

Every word my mom ever said to me, her actions, and every aspect of her life that at one point hurt me, today move me with great compassion. I don't want to cause her to hurt any more than she already has, only God knows the things that she's been through since she was a child. Nothing gives me the right to add to her pain. My parents have unresolved issues that they still need to deal with and for years the devil's plan has been to separate them, but I know deep inside my heart that God kept them together because He is bigger and greater than any issue in their lives.

As my prayer life became the source of my peace, I determined in my heart to love her no matter what. Love covers a multitude of sins and I wanted to bring peace to our relationship. It was in the process of learning to love her and to accept her as who she is that I learned the true meaning of honor. I discovered that I was to respect my mother no matter what and nothing gave me the excuse to talk back to her or about her.

Since they retired several years ago, they have been visiting us every summer and I love to have them, especially lately because I reconciled with them. Here are some notes from my journals that I wrote during those visits,

Journal notes:

My parents have been here since Wednesday. My mom managed to press a couple of my buttons that could've ended in an argument, but God had a hold on me. The pastor preached about "the peace of God" today, and thank the Lord I have such peace. I was just thinking about the things I heard today, especially from my mom…Lord, help me not to judge her, help me to love her in spite of her tongue. Help me to show her the Jesus in me. I trust you, Lord.

*****

Lord, help me to endure my mother's weaknesses, her negative talk, her selfish ways, her judging mouth. Lord help me to love her even when I don't feel like it. Help me to never have a grudge against her. You are my strength, you are my shield, you are my fortress, you are my everything!

Today I realized that I must bring up my daughter in the fear of the Lord, for there is no other way.

The fear of the Lord makes you wise and gives you understanding. The fear of the Lord is perfect. The fear of the Lord takes you on the path of righteousness. The fear of the Lord gives life and long days in the land which the Lord has given you. The fear of the Lord helps you to love and submit. The fear of the Lord gives you hope for a future that God holds in His hands. The fear of the Lord is the first step toward a relationship with Him. The fear of the Lord is pure, undefiled love and hope. Only by the fear of the Lord we will see all His goodness, because He is perfect, He desires for us to be perfect.

Thank you, Lord, for teaching me the fear of you.

*****

Yesterday, I spoke to my mom and for the first time in my life, I felt that she truly has the spirit of God within her. She asked me to forgive her for her selfishness, she realized that she only thought about herself without giving so much thought to the way we were growing up. Only God can make her see the reality of things. Only God can open her eyes to the truth. I cried because for the first time I felt that I had a mother who actually cares about me.

Lord, thank you for the work that you are doing in her life, thank you for teaching me your word day by day and for reassuring me of your love. I trust you!

*****

My parents left this morning. Their stay seemed brief although they were here for six weeks. All along their stay I went with Proverbs 10:12. "Hatred stirs up strife, but love covers all sins."

Lord, only you are the fountain of life, of strength and of power! Your word is truth. I love my parents so very much and this time around, I expressed my love for them and overlooked all their weaknesses. Thank you, Father, for only you allowed me to share the love of Jesus in my heart. Love is the bond of perfection. Jesus is love and peace and joy and only if I have Him, I can express His love. Thank you, Lord.

Today, I truly understand not only the concept of love but the true meaning of honor. I will miss my parents greatly, but now I feel closer to them than ever before, the distance won't matter because love is in my heart.

Lord, bless my parents. Heal their marriage and lead them in love and in truth to follow you! Thank you, Father, for I know it is done!

As my relationship with the Lord grew, my love for my parents grew. Love is the bond of perfection and because I was able to give them love, I now have a better relationship with them. My mother and I became closer and I found out that I can actually learn some things from her because I chose love over judgment. I realize that every time her conduct gives way to rage, it is because of the pain she suffered in the past, and her decision to keep it to herself and not fully submit it to the Lord. But I constantly remind myself that I'm not here to judge, nor criticize. I'm here to love.

The true meaning of God's commandment to honor my parents is doing the right thing, no matter what the circumstances. I have to honor my parents because it is obeying God's fifth commandment. I don't have to approve of the things they say and do, even when they hurt me. I just have to love and respect them because God commanded it. Will I question God?

We only have two earthly parents. They may not be our favorite people in the world. We might even think that they don't deserve our love and respect, but this doesn't matter because if God gave a commandment with a promise, our job is to obey the Lord's commandment. Everything that Jesus came to teach is a manual for our wellbeing. Every commandment has a purpose and obeying God only leads us to be blessed by Him who knows better and who leads us to life and life more abundantly.

Prayer has been key in restoring my relationship with my parents. Life is better when we pray; it is peaceful, it is sweeter and it is more meaningful when we pray. Pray your care and watch the Lord work in your life.

Ask, and it will be given to you; seek, and you will find; knock and the door will be opened to you.

For everyone who asks receives; the one who seeks finds; and to the one who knocks, the door will be opened.

Luke 11:9-10 (NIV)

Becoming One

...and they shall become one... (Genesis 2:24)

When I married my husband, I knew that I loved him with all of my heart and that I wanted us to spend the rest of our lives together. What I didn't know is that there were lots of issues that we needed to work on to be on the same page. God saw that in order for us to become one, we would have to have the same mind. Our characters were completely different. We had different opinions and views in life. Even our taste buds were different. We were opposites in many ways but our hearts longed for each other.

When God came into our lives, He came to work out all those things that would make us distant from each other. I cannot say it has been easy, especially for me, because I had to learn to submit and let go of many fears, but the Lord is patient and thanks to Him, my husband is also.

When my daughter was still very little, we had a heated argument in his aunt's house. I don't remember the details, but we hurt each other and at the end of it all, I recall telling him, "Why did we argue so much and said so many hurtful things?" I think that day we saw a glimpse of how words can be more like knives to our hearts.

The devil always tried to plant seeds of doubt, bitterness, and unforgiveness in my heart, but I did not let him. I resisted him by staying steadfast in my faith, knowing that my Father was in control of all things. I know that he also tried to do the same thing with my husband. At one point, when our fights were at the peak of its season, he said some things to me that wounded my heart. I forgave him and gave it all to the Lord and I let Him heal me. Many more times, he hurt me and even when he never apologized, I forgave him right away. Why hold a grudge and let the devil have his way? I love my husband and I know that he loves me too.

In the last couple of years, God always pointed me to read a scripture in Zechariah which says not to think evil in your heart toward anyone (see 8:17). I always chose to believe the best especially when it comes to my husband. I never tried to read in between the lines, even when things got bad. I chose to trust him. In prayer, I approached the One who is able to fix all things, solve all things, and work all things out for our benefit. I let Him fight my battles for me, and I did not lose heart because I put my trust in God. I knew that He was able to restore broken people, broken families, and work in our lives if we submitted ourselves to Him. We chose to let Him work in our lives. We were committed to each other and determined to make things work as a family.

Journal notes:
Today I had a big argument with my husband. After all was said and done, I realized that the devil will use anything to break our peace, he is in to steal any bit of joy that we may have. But I have decided that it is God who fights all our battles for us and that I will not give in to his schemes. I will not have him steal my peace, my joy, or anything else. God will have the final say.

I trust you, Lord! It doesn't matter what comes against me, I trust you! I know that you love me. I know that you have good plans for my life and I choose to follow you and to submit every area of my life to you. I will not be so easily offended. I will not listen to the lies of the devil. I trust you! My hope is in you, my strength is in you. Whatever the devil intends for evil, you will turn it into good. You are faithful.

Forgive me if I was judgmental. Forgive my husband for his proudful ways, I know you are working in him, and the work that you have started in us, you will bring to completion until the day of Jesus Christ.

*****

The last couple of days have been tough. After seeing my husband's reaction on Sunday on our way to his mom's, I got very emotional. The enemy whispered a few lies on my ear, and although I got weak for a little while, then I got strong.

I am founded, established and settled on a rock which is Jesus Christ and I will not allow the enemy to come and try to destroy what took years to build. I know that God is for me, I know He loves me no matter what and He who is in me is stronger than he who is in the world. I will prevail, my family will stand strong and faithful. I rebuke the enemy and his lies, he is a liar and a thief and I will not let him rob me of the peace that Jesus died for me to have. I will not, I will not!

*****

I am very sad. Bernie said some things this morning that deeply hurt me and this evening he decided to ignore me. What is causing this behavior in him? I don't know...

Lord, you are God and I trust You. I know that all things are in your hands. I pray that you keep my family whole and healthy. I pray that we may be able to stand strong in You. I love my husband. I know you are here in the midst of us, in our marriage, in our family. Thank You that no weapon formed against us will prosper. Please help me to remain humble and submissive. Help me to do your will and to open my mouth only to bless. Help me to be strong and not to take any offenses to heart, but to grow in You. Lead me and guide me, you are my strength.

*****

Bernie came tonight still angry at me. He said I attacked him early in the morning, did I? My daughter started crying because she doesn't like it when we argue. It breaks my heart to see her cry. For a moment I felt very angry at him, he won't let go of his anger and resentment. I cried too, but then I calmed myself down because I will not let the enemy win. I love my husband and even if I don't like his behavior, I won't judge him. I will not say anything else about the subject. I am hurt but I will let go and I will let God work it out. I trust in the Lord with all of my heart.

Times like this is where I have to stand strong on my Rock, Jesus Christ. I will not move. My peace remains because it comes from Him. This is not a battle with my husband, it is a battle with the enemy that stands between us, and he is a defeated foe. God's got my back. I stand, Lord, I stand.

*****

Two days ago, I got into an argument with my husband over something I said that made him upset. I defended myself for a minute and after pausing and listening to that still, small voice I heard, "Don't defend yourself, let the Lord do it, give the other cheek." I said nothing else and I apologized and peace came. When I gave it to God, when I entered His rest, I got *peace.* As soon as I started praying in the spirit, my husband came and hugged me and said, "I don't want us fighting any more, I don't want our daughter to grow up the way you did." I see it now, only God could give him a revelation like that.

I grew up with two parents who fought every day and I recall not liking it at all. Affliction will not rise up a second time (Nahum 1:9).

Thank you, Lord!

Every fight I had with my husband was a test for me to see how I would react. At times I passed the test, other times I felt like a victim and I felt bad and mistreated. Yet other times I was humbled not only by my husband, but by God Himself. I got to see what was in my heart and it was not pretty.

Bernie has always seen the real issue in me—my fears—and he hates it when I give in to the lies of the enemy. More than a couple of times he said to me, "I can't change you, only God can." My immediate thought after he made such a statement was, *Why would you want to change me, can't you accept me the way I am?* That sounded like a fair thought to have, but it wasn't because I didn't have a clear vision of what he saw in me. After much prayer and meditation, I realized that God is working in me through him. I have to learn to understand that there are real issues that need to be addressed in me to attain the level of freedom from fear that the Lord wants me to have.

Unfortunately, many of our fights have been linked to vocalizing my fears. My husband's desire has always been for me to change the thoughts of fear that I allow to come in and entertain in my mind; not the way I am, but the way I let myself be when I'm deceived by the devil and tempted to fear. My vulnerability to fear is my weakness and he saw it before I ever did.

I have learned that if I want my marriage to thrive, I have to submit and obey. I cannot be on one page and my husband in another. Opposition has always been the devil's insurance to defeat us. Every time I oppose my husband, I become disobedient not only to him, but to God's commandment to submit to my husband. We have to think alike. Jesus said in Matthew 12, "Every house divided against itself will not stand." I looked at this verse of scripture time and time again in the last couple of years. Every word that Jesus said in this verse is related to how I have to stand in my own house. If I am going to allow my husband and I to become enemies by being against each other, then I open the door to the devil to come into my house and do his job and destroy our family. He is clever enough to mask himself as an angel of light and then he attacks.

The devil's target is to destroy anything that the Lord wants to bless in our lives. He creates a hostile environment in our homes because he only knows to do what he does best, which is to steal, kill and to destroy (see John 10:10). God wants our families to remain together so He can work in our lives. He is interested in raising people to honor and glorify His name. He wants unity in our families because He seeks godly offspring (see Malachi 2:15).

I found out that in times of distress, I have to dig out the things that I know. What do I know? I know that my husband loves me. He may not be acting like he does sometimes, he might snap and say things to hurt me, but I know that he loves me. We all say things we don't mean to say in a moment of anger, yet it doesn't mean we don't love. Times of testing and conflict come and go, and it is in those times that I speak God's word out loud and fight the good fight of faith. Everything that I have studied and memorized suddenly comes back when I need it the most and it is what keeps me strong, knowing that God is with me regardless of the circumstances around me. He gives me confidence and peace. Wisdom and knowledge become the stability of my times. (see Isaiah 33:6)

What I have learned in over twenty years of marriage is that you don't give up on your husband because he has said or has done things that hurt you. I have learned to pray for him and in prayer, I have learned to forgive. It is not easy to let go and to let God handle things in our relationship, but I found out that the times I have let God handle our differences, we have gotten closer to each other. I love my husband and I know that God's plan is for our good as we continue to become one.

I believe that God will work all things out for us as He already has. There are no perfect marriages but there are couples willing to let God work in their lives. Only He can restore, heal, and bring life to broken hearts. All things are possible if we believe. I chose to believe and God never failed me.

Our marriage has been a work in progress since the beginning. We are becoming one in the path of knowing and trusting each other, and it takes work, commitment, endurance, faith, hope, love, and prayer. The moment I said "I do," I committed myself to work at it, to be patient, to have faith, to hope all things, and to love always, even when I don't feel like it. But one thing I know is that everything works better with God in it. I am able to love with true love when the One who is love is living within me.

Wives, submit to your own husbands, as to the Lord. Husbands, love your wives, just as Christ loved the church and gave himself for her.
Ephesians 5:22,25

Don't Worry, Don't Be Anxious, Don't Be Afraid

"In the multitude of my anxieties within me, your comforts delight my soul" (Psalm 94:19).

Have you ever been worried to the point of feeling sick? Have you ever thought the worst possible outcome of the situation you saw yourself in? I know I have. I felt sick to my stomach, dizzy and ready to vomit with the anticipation of what might happen. But after I felt this way, nothing changed. The devil used every possible thought of every possible worst-case scenario and it made me feel even worse.

One evening, my husband called me from work to advise me that he could not find his phone and that he was going to be coming home. Right after I hang up with him, my mother-in-law called me to ask me about him —he usually calls her about the same time or earlier every day. I innocently told her about the lost phone situation and reassured her that he would call her when he got home.

Less than an hour later, she called again to ask me if my husband got home and she sounded worried sick. I sensed the spirit of worry and I despised it and then it clicked! I completely forgot that my mother-in-law is a hard-core worrier; she can make anyone around her raise their blood pressure in just seconds with fear and dread of the worst possible scenario.

My husband got home just as I hang up the phone with her, and as soon as I told him that his mom knew about his missing phone, he got upset with me. He questioned what caused me to tell her anything knowing that she worries about everything. Great! Not only did I cause her to worry but I also provoked him to stress! I tried to explain that I did not mean to tell her anything but he would not hear what I had to say, so I quickly walked away from him because I knew that I could not justify myself.

My husband reminded me that if I lost my phone I would panic also—and I have—and unfortunately every time I panic, I sense my blood rushing to my head. This is the kind of stress I don't wish nor desire to have, and neither should anyone.

Not long ago, I woke up when it was still dark and I did not recall turning off my phone, so I got up and went to look for it. I couldn't find it anywhere and I remembered last seeing it in the car that was parked outside the house. I did not want to go outside in the dark and the enemy tried to fill my mind with doubt and worry, but I decided that I was going to go back to sleep and not worry. This was not as easy as it sounds. I made myself go back to sleep and stopped the worry from coming in. I learned not to worry, but it doesn't come naturally. We are only human, we tend to panic and worry about the smallest things, and that leads to stress that I try to avoid at all costs because I simply don't like the way I feel when I let worry take a hold of me.

The truth is that when we worry, we do not believe that God is able to work in us to fulfill His will in our lives, we attract the negative and we cause the very thing that we are fearing to come to life. Job said, "For the thing that I greatly feared has come upon me, and what I dreaded has happened to me" (Job 3:25).

A couple of years ago, on one of our visits to my mother-in-law, I sent my husband on an errand to buy take-out food. The restaurant was probably about five blocks away in NYC, but my husband does not like to rush, so he probably took his time walking because he was gone for just under an hour. I recall my mother-in-law walking back and forth and I sensed her uneasiness all the time that he was gone. She slowly approached me with deep worry in her countenance as she asked me, "Where is he, why is he taking so long?" I remember the feeling I had and I did not like it at all. I tried to calm her down and I said, "He's probably on his way."

Fear is an ugly, uncomfortable, and dreadful feeling! It is binding and debilitating. It takes away hope and joy and it is to be avoided at all costs. It is also very contagious. For a moment, the devil wanted me to fear and have the kind of fear that was in her, but I did not let him because I knew better. I had heard his lies for very many years and I saw how fear got the best of my life. My husband came back home just minutes later and we sat down to enjoy our meal.

I am not going to say that I don't ever worry because it would not be true, but I will tell you that when I see worry creep in, I resist it with everything I've got. I often silence the voice of the enemy by praying and speaking scripture out loud. The devil is a liar and the father of it. His job is to make us think that impending doom is right around the corner. He does his job effectively and he knows how to get our mind to actually picture the events live. God's word says to resist the devil and he will flee (James 4:7).

Journal notes:

A couple of days ago, I had a heated argument with my husband. Het got very upset because I called him selfish. Why did I call him selfish? I had made a juice for him to drink and he didn't like it very much; actually, I had three cups for him to choose from with different juices. I remember calling him selfish because I had made him the juices thinking about his health and the fact that he didn't want to drink it made me think about how he is only concerned about his taste buds and not his overall health.

My husband said some very hurtful things to me, he called me wicked and then he said he didn't want to be around me. This really hurt. I had a temper tantrum and I stormed out the room and went upstairs to find God. I admit I let worry creep in and it was wrong. I asked the Lord to forgive me. Just earlier that day, I had meditated on scriptures to keep my mouth shut, but of course I didn't. I clearly recall hearing in my spirit, "I will heal him, not the juice." My biggest mistake was to think that I can fix his health with the juice I wanted him to drink.

What have I learned today? I can't do anything on my own, so why worry? Why fight a battle that is not mine?

Lord help me to honor you with my mouth. Lead me and guide me to be a good wife and a good mother, to speak words of life and to fear not because You are always with me. Thank You, Father!

When I read this, the whole incident came back to me as if it was yesterday. I learned not to worry about the things I have no control over. Prior to this incident, my husband had a blood test that showed that his sugar and cholesterol levels were high. I always liked juicing and I thought to myself, "If I could just get him to drink these juices, his health will improve." I worried and my mistake was to give in to fear.

This had to happen in order for me to understand that God is in control of all things, not me. My job is to care for my husband and not to stress him. In fact, the stress I caused him that day gave him a headache. Every time we argue his body responds with a migraine. I learned to give it to God and let Him take care of things. I prayed for my husband to be healthy and for him to learn to like the meals that I prepared for him. That is all I am supposed to do and I do it to the best of my ability. In the weeks to come, his attitude started changing. I did not push on him anything that he didn't want to eat or drink. I didn't even offer him a smoothie anymore. This is what I wrote a couple of months later:

Journal notes:
This morning, Bernie was watching a program about beets and beet juice and he mentioned he would like one. For the first

time after our juice incident, I gave him a juice and he said he liked it. Halleluiah!

Thank you, Father, for I know You work all things out. I realized that I can't under any circumstances do anything on my own. You are the potter and we are the clay, we are but the work of Your hands.

One big argument caused me to see what lies secretly within my heart. Worry is fear, fear is unbelief, and unbelief is not trusting God. I am determined to trust more and worry less.

"How long must I wrestle with my thoughts and day after day have sorrows in my heart? How long will my enemy triumph over me?" (Psalm 13:2 NIV)

It's was a wonderful day and the weather couldn't be better as I found myself trying to decide whether to go out or not. Tired of sitting on the fence, I decided to ask God to lead me by His word and I opened my Bible to Psalm 13:2 and I immediately knew that the Lord was speaking to me in plain simple words, "How long?" How long will I live anxious about making the smallest decisions? How long will fear of everything dominate my mind? How long will the enemy lie to me?

The things that make me anxious may not be the same things that make someone else anxious; we all have strengths and weaknesses in different areas of our lives. There was a period in my life when money or rather the lack of it made me anxious. I remember times when I had several bills due at the same time and not having enough resources to pay for it all drove me to the point of desperation and anxiety, so much so that it started interfering with my physical wellbeing. Stress is the outcome of frustration on matters that we have no control over.

I believe that we should fix what we can, but there are things that are out of our control and it is those things that we must learn to submit to God and say, *"Lord, I know what I am capable of doing and I know that there are things that are simply out of my control. You take over the things that I cannot control and give me the peace of knowing that I am in the palm of Your hands and that this is not a problem for You."*

In my walk with the Lord, I have learned to make prayers like this. The things that steal my peace are the weapons that the enemy uses to cause me to be anxious. When anxiety becomes my burden, I know that the word of God is powerful enough to get me through anything. I often remind God of His promises because prayer is a powerful weapon to gain back my peace.

How long will the enemy triumph over me? The answer is very simple, as long as I remain ignorant of his schemes. He is a deceiver and he has studied each and every one of us better than anyone else. He knows what makes us upset, he knows what bothers us, he knows what buttons to push to make us angry, he basically knows us better than we know ourselves and he will stop at nothing to push us to the edge. The things that we ignore are the things that make us vulnerable to him. Wisdom is priceless and we are to seek it more than anything else. Wisdom is the beginning of knowledge and it promotes us in ways we could never imagine.

One of my favorite verses in the Bible is when Jesus visits the house of Mary and Martha. Can you make a mental picture of what happened that day? Martha invites Jesus into her house, lets Him in and she rushes to the kitchen to prepare food. Meanwhile, Mary sits right beside Him; she is drawn to His presence where she feels at peace. She has decided that the best thing for her to do is to listen to what He has to say. But Martha is distracted and burdened with much serving and she approached Jesus to ask Him to tell her sister to help her, but Jesus responds,

"Martha, Martha, you are worried and troubled about many things, but one thing is needed, and Mary has cho-

sen that part, which will not be taken away from her" (Luke 10:41-42).

Jesus knew what was in Martha's heart and He explained that Mary had chosen the right thing to do. Martha invited Jesus to serve Him with food, yet she did not realize that Jesus came to serve and the words that were coming out of His mouth were the real food that was being served in her house that day.

Isn't this a picture of us when we invite Jesus to live in our hearts and then we get too busy to spend time with Him? I speak out of my own experiences because it has happened to me. Distracted by work, daily chores and routine, I found myself having no time to spend with Him resulting in my own exhaustion, anxiety, depression, and fear. For years, fear got the best of me and it affected my physical well-being as well as my spiritual one. Jesus came to show all of us to live more abundantly. The life that He offers is far greater and better than anything we ever dreamed about. He is the source of our life. In His presence, we learn about the life that He has intended for us to live. For me, one of the most rewarding experiences is to sit and be quiet in the presence of the Lord. He is the source of my peace and in His presence, I find it.

Next time anxiety comes uninvited, as it has often come into my life, meditate on God's promises and pray for His peace, the peace of God which surpasses all understanding. Don't let the enemy step into your life and rob you of one inch of your precious peace. God Himself is our peace. He is the source of our joy. When life has become overwhelming and things that make you anxious keep piling up stealing your peace, your joy and even your sleep, perhaps it's time to stop and pray,

Lord, I know that You are in control of all things and the things that are robbing me of my peace are nothing for you. I realize that no matter what happens, you have me in the palm of your hands. Please help me to see beyond my fears and anxieties. Give me Your peace and help me trust that You are working in my life. You will work out your purpose in my life.

The Lord will perfect that which concerns me.
Psalm 138:8

The Core of Life is Death

"I no longer live, but Christ lives in me"
(Galatians 2:20 NIV).

My prayer life was born out of adversity and fear. All the things that happened in my life, all the trials, the lack, the attacks of the devil, it all led me to pray. On my knees I learned to look up higher. I gave all my burdens to Him who is able to work in me to transform me into the likeness of His Son Jesus. In His presence I learned to value the things that matter most in this life; what money cannot buy is indeed priceless.

There are choices we make, and prayer is one of them. Prayer is the sole foundation of living in the fear of the Lord. When we pray, we not only acknowledge God, we also become aware that we are not able to do anything outside of ourselves; we are dependent on

Him in every aspect of our lives. He is God alone. He created the heavens and the earth and everything in it.

"The heavens declare the glory of God; the skies proclaim the work of his hands" (Psalm 19:1 NIV).

The Lord has a word for us every day and it is up to us to receive it or not. I picture Him handing us our daily spiritual bread as we seek His face and I know that He longs for us to receive it. He wants us to live fulfilled, worry-free, fearless, blessed and empowered lives, but it all begins with prayer.

The knowledge I get comes from Him and it's usually given to me when I wholeheartedly seek Him, knowing and believing that in Him are all my answers because He is God. I was going through my very first journal and in it I found notes of things that I should've learned then but I didn't. I took notes of the things I heard. Every sermon I ever heard became my lesson, but I wasn't recording it in my mind and heart, it was all just in paper.

We can sit in church and hear the pastor preach, but when the service is over, we walk out as empty as we came. We go home and real life wipes away everything we just learned at church. This is exactly what happened to me in the beginning of my walk with God. I used to go to church Sunday for morning and evening services, Tuesday morning for prayer, Wednesday evening for mid-week service, Thursday morning for prayer, Friday evening for fellowship, and sometimes even Saturday for other events. With this much church, you'd think I knew enough to become a spiritual giant, but I didn't. I was going to church and yes, I was learning, but I was not applying enough of it into my life. All the notes I made did not make me knowledgeable nor ready to apply what I learned into my life. Do you know what did? The trials, the tests, and the uncomfortable situations that came into my life are what caused me to apply God's word to my life.

My husband has been an instrument of God's work in my life. He is bold and does not hesitate to tell me the things that need to change in me. I remember one day when we were at the supermarket and I was thinking about whether to get an item or not. I was being economical but I was also afraid of spending money. My husband came around and he asked me if I got it and I said no because I wanted to wait until it was on sale. He got very upset and he said, "Stop your misery!" For a moment I got upset, then embarrassed, then I composed myself. I knew that, once again, the fear of not having enough had taken a hold of me. My husband saw my fear, and perhaps through him, God was teaching me to keep that fear away.

Journal notes:

Yesterday my husband got upset with me because I was not ready on time to go to church. He made me hear his opinion on the whole matter; he was tough! At first, I thought he was being mean and temperamental, but he made a point when he said, "Put God first! If you had to go to a job, you would be ready on time. Respect the Man above!"

I knew that God was using him to make a point that needed to be made. I must be organized enough to be ready and on time for church on Sundays. My husband saw that I was taking it lightly and he made a point which I saw like I never did before.

I recognize the work that the Lord is doing in me, even in small things. He is changing my heart, my mind, and my ways. He takes His time to complete His work. He is not in a rush to get me from point A to point B, because He is more concerned about working on one thing at a time and in perfecting His work in me. I have learned that the Lord will use anything and anyone to let me see what needs to change in my life.

This morning, I walked into my kitchen and I saw that my husband and my daughter used up all the cups and plates, and they left it all for me to clean up. My first reaction was to get upset and maybe I did for a second or so. Then I reminded myself that I am here to serve and getting upset will not change anything. As a matter of fact, I can create a conflict if I open my mouth to complain. So, I decided to quickly clean up everything and make the most of it, and I felt at peace when I decided to do this.

I also remind myself that I will have to go through the same mountain over and over again until I learn to keep a joyful attitude. My trials may be as insignificant as a pile of dirty dishes, but those little things are working for me to attain a character that will please God. I don't have to always understand what He is up to; my job is to trust Him and let Him complete His work in me. I trust Him enough to understand that in order for me to learn something, He will put me through whatever is necessary for me to go through.

I think that at some point or another, we all forget that we are here for a reason. I know that it happened to me. There was a stage in my life that I was complaining about all the work that I had to do in my house, I never thought for a moment that God puts us in specific places to serve one another. He gave me a husband and a daughter to care for, but at one point in my life, I forgot that the one being blessed by serving them and caring for them was me. I saw it as a burden when my husband didn't clean up and always waited for me to do everything, I was more concerned about what he wasn't doing than enjoying the labor of love that I was supposed to be doing for him. When my attitude changed, everything changed, and today I feel blessed to have such a wonderful family and to be able to care for them.

When God took a hold of me, He taught me that learning comes with hands-on practice. You don't graduate from college and become the president of a company, you move up on the ladder of success. The more reliable you prove yourself, the sooner you'll get promoted. I discovered that God used the same method to work in my life.

When I think about all the things that God has done and continues to do for me, I get very emotional because I see the work that He has been doing in me. Today I am not the same person I was a year ago and perhaps even the same person that I was a week ago. God has allowed me to grow and mature in the very areas that were difficult for me. I am not a spiritual baby anymore, but I'm not fully mature either; I realize that I still have a long way to go.

Our sanctification is a lifelong process, but the results are peace and joy in the Lord. God's word is so powerful that He is able to change our lives for the better. Jesus said that all things are possible if we believe. God with us, God for us, God in us.

> *For through the law I died to the law, so that I might live for God. I have been crucified with Christ and I no longer live but Christ lives in me. The life I now live in the body, I live by faith in the Son of God, who loved me and gave himself for me.*
>
> Galatians 2:19-20 (NIV)

Journal notes:
I believe that the thought "the core of life is death," was given to me by God. He wants to teach me something that I will learn only if I want to. I remembered that every time I would try to teach my daughter something new, it wouldn't work for her benefit unless she really wanted to learn it from her heart, and it was mainly math lessons. God will teach me only as much as I let Him teach me. Wisdom will be mine in the degree I want to acquire it.

Lord, help me to grasp your teaching. What are you showing me? Give me wisdom to understand your teaching. I trust you!
*****

It is shortly before 5:00 a.m. and I woke up to thunder. Lord, you are God and you are good. Thank you for loving me enough to wake me up to meditate on your word. You are an awesome God.

It's like a voice played on my mind all night long, "I no longer live, but Christ lives in me."

Christ lives in me... Christ lives in me... He lives in me! It took me a very long time to understand that my life belongs to the Lord. I don't think we fully understand that when we receive Christ into our hearts as our Lord and Savior, He comes to dwell in us. I know I didn't. Perhaps it's a control issue. I wanted to be in charge of my life and everything in it. I didn't want anyone to come into my life and tell me what to do. I used to call out to God when I needed Him, but I did not allow Him to rule over my thoughts, my actions, and my mouth. I wanted to be in charge of those things.

If I can illustrate what Jesus does when He comes onto our lives, it is like when we move into a new house, we walk in to clean up and change everything that the previous owners left in it. We fix it to our taste, decorate it with our own style, and then we maintain it the way we like it. This is exactly what Jesus comes to do in our lives. When He comes to live in our hearts, He cleans house and everything that needs to go will go because if He is living in our house, He will ensure that we are living up to His standards. Otherwise things will get uncomfortable.

This is exactly what happened to me after our move to Connecticut. God manifested His presence in my life and He did a complete renovation of my heart, mind, and soul. He showed me the attitudes that needed to go, the behaviors that needed to change and the fears that I needed to confront. Can I say His work is done in me? Absolutely not! Just when I thought I mastered something, He showed me something else that needs to change.

Years ago, as I was having an argument with my husband, I let fear of the things that concerned me regarding our finances get the best of me. My husband was doing the best he could and I felt as if I failed him. I made him feel bad. My attitude was wrong as I was arrogant and prideful with my speech.

I noticed that if I just focus on everything that is wrong, it leaves no room for the things that are right, and for the things that matter the most. Unfortunately for me, my heart was not set on the Lord nor the efforts that my husband was making for us, but on the things that bothered me. I was so sorry for it. I let pride in and it caused me to become someone I didn't want to be. I was not living by faith and without faith, it is impossible to please the Lord.

"When my heart is overwhelmed, lead me to the rock that is higher than I" (Psalm 61:2).

I realized that if I can see my mistakes, I have accomplished something good. If I was going to grow up, I needed to see what was in my heart. I needed to see the pride and any other behavior that needed to change in me. In His mercy, God allowed me to see what lies deep within my heart. Those behaviors and traits that brought a negative effect to my own environment were the things that I wanted to get rid of. The changes that I thought were impossible to accomplish were accomplished by prayer and submission to God. We become more like Jesus when we let Him work in every aspect of our lives.

Every experience helped me to watch the way I live and the things I say. I'm especially careful not to complain. Because I was able to see what needed to change in me, I decided that every day I would write a list of things to be grateful for. Being thankful helps me to focus on the things that are most important. It is harder to complain when you recognize the things you do have and are grateful for. When I feel like complaining, I choose to give thanks. When I get angry I recognize that I need to spend more time with the Lord. When fear comes knocking at my door, I pray the living word. God has become my go-to person for my every need.

Walking in the fear of the Lord is discerning His will and becoming humble enough to let Him complete His work in me. Because Jesus died for me, I will now live for Him. I will live to give Him honor and praise in everything I say, do, and think. I know I can do nothing out of my own strength, but by His Spirit I can allow the One who lives in me to work in my life, to do, and to act in order to fulfill His good purpose in my life (see Philippians 2:13).

"Fill me with the knowledge of Your will" (Colossians 1:9).

Did you ever ask God, "Lord, what is your will for my life?" I believe I have asked this question many times in the last couple of years, but I don't think I really wanted to hear what God had to say to me, not if it involved change and getting me out of my comfort zone. I know I am not alone, even Moses felt that he was not equipped to do what God asked him to do.

When God appeared to him, I don't think it ever crossed his mind that God would ask him to get His people out of Israel.

> *Please, Lord, I have never been eloquent—either in the past or recently or since you have been speaking to your servant—because I am slow*

and hesitant in speech...Please, Lord, send someone else.

Exodus 4:10,13 (HCSB)

God reminded Moses that He made the human mouth and that he was going to help him speak, but this didn't prevent Moses from resisting. He did not want to be the one for the job. Perhaps, he didn't believe enough in himself and he thought that being slow in speech put him at a disadvantage. Jonah, on the other hand, decided to take a boat in a different direction when God asked him to go to Nineveh, until he found himself in the belly of a fish.

Many years ago, I heard a word on writing a book on the fear of the Lord, but I didn't think much of it. However, it was always in the back of my mind. I studied the fear of the Lord and this led me to know Him more. I spent long periods of time in the presence of the Lord and I wrote letters to Him in my journals for many years not knowing or understanding that He was working in me and equipping me to take the job.

I never thought writing would be my calling. All these years, I always knew deep inside my heart that God was preparing me for something, but it never crossed my mind that writing would be it. I went through many phases in my life and many times when I thought to myself, what am I doing? I spent long periods of doing nothing not realizing that all along the Lord was working in my life to mold me and lead me to do His will.

Journal notes:
Today is my husband's birthday. Today is also the birth of what the rest of my life will be like. I said a few things to my husband last night, and what followed humbled me and made me realize that I need to wake up. In a few sentences, my husband gave me a visual of what my life has been like, I never saw it like that.

It is time to wake up! I cried out to the Lord and He heard me. He answered my prayers and showed me things that I never understood before. Through His word, I hear His voice loud and clear. Last night I asked Him to show me His will for my life. Years ago, I believe I heard in my spirit, "Write a book on the fear of the Lord." Was this really the voice of God asking me to do this? How could I make sure? I prayed and I asked God to talk to me today about writing a book. We went to church and I thought, "Perhaps I will hear it there." As we were coming back, in the car, my husband said, "I bought a computer for you to write a book and that's what you should do."

Just in case I was not convinced that this was the will of God for my life, days later I came across the scripture where Jesus said,

> *"Not everyone who says to Me 'Lord, Lord,' will enter the kingdom of heaven, but only the one who does the will of my Father who is in heaven"* (Matthew 7:21 NIV).

After I read this scripture, the fear of God got deep inside my heart and soul. Sooner rather than later, I had to come face to face with His calling and stopped running away from the work that He has called me to do. All these years, in trials, fears and uncertainties, I've been learning to trust God's leading in my life. Now is the time when I must step out of my comfort zone and walk by faith to do the work that the Lord wants me to do.

One step a time, one day at a time, and under His leading, I will trust in the Lord. I will do the work that He has called me to do. I know that He is pleased when I know that the plans that He has for me are for good. Whatever task is in front of me will be accomplished because He has already given me the grace to succeed. I will walk in obedience knowing that my steps are ordered by the Lord and therefore, I will not fear.

The Holy Spirit comes to help us become Christlike, to help us in whatever situation we might be in. We are here to complete the work that the Lord has assigned for us to do. My assignment is not going to be the same as my neighbor's, my assignment is exclusively for me.

In the same way that God entrusted me to care for my daughter and for my husband, He has entrusted me to care for the assignment that He has given me to do.

This morning after I read my Bible, I left it opened in the book of Acts 1 and I highlighted verse eight, "...you will receive power when the Holy Spirit comes on you..." Later in the evening, as I was on the phone dealing with an issue, I went to get my organizer from my desk and my husband commented that the scripture that I had highlighted is powerful. What am I trying to say? The word of God is living and it can touch the life of anyone and at any moment.

I cannot comprehend many things. I do not understand completely the way God works in my life or in the life of those around me, and maybe I will never understand His ways. But one thing I know, God is continually working in my life, every day, every hour, every minute and every second. I know that I am walking in the spirit because the moment I received Him into my life, He came to dwell in my heart and the more I get to know Him, the more He reminds me that it is He who is works in me and not I in myself.

Walking with the Lord has made me humble. I know what joy feels like and I know where my strength comes from—it's only found in the Lord. If I can tell you what I have learned in life up to this point in a few words, I can tell you that I have learned to pray and to fear God. Only He is worthy of our fear because we depend on Him for our everything in life.

Last year, I shared with my parents that I read *The Cross and the Switchblade* by David Wilkerson and the one thing that touched me the most was his decision to spend time with God. It was during his time of devotions and prayer that he found God's will for his life. One decision changed the outcome of his entire life and reached millions of people who were being deceived by the enemy into self-destruction. One choice. One God. One decision. One ministry with millions of lives saved. This is the power of the Gospel of Jesus Christ.

After reading inspiring books and spending time with the Lord, I finally understand that when our journey in this life is over, only what was done for Jesus will count, for He said:

> *Do not lay up for yourselves treasures on earth, where moth and rust destroy and where thieves break in and steal; but lay up for yourselves treasures in heaven, where neither moth nor rust destroys and where thieves do not break in and steal. For where your treasure is, there your heart will be also.*
>
> *Mathew 6:19-21*

I can spend the rest of my life chasing fantasies, money, or fame, but when all is said and done, I will only be fulfilled by what I have accomplished for God. Walking in the fear of the Lord is accomplishing His will in my life and becoming the woman that I was born to be.

Jesus came to give us a great commission and spread the gospel of good news to the world. Most of us will not go unto all the world witnessing for Jesus, but we can do it right where we are planted, beginning in our homes, and it begins with prayer. We can live out our faith in front of our children, our family, and friends and win souls for God's kingdom. We can share the things that God is doing in our lives and give a testimony of His goodness and mercy. We are here with a purpose and that is to show His love and His faithfulness to everyone. It starts with one decision, to believe in Jesus and to accept Him into our hearts to change our lives for His honor and glory.

It is time to wake up and pray and win souls for the kingdom of God. It is time to hear His voice and His calling. It is time to live for the Lord. No regrets, no fears, no doubts. Submitted to His will. Nourished by His love. Empowered by His spirit. Surrounded by His favor. Equipped by His word. Focused on Jesus, the author and the finisher of our faith.

Pray your care and watch Him work in your life.

CPSIA information can be obtained
at www.ICGtesting.com
Printed in the USA
LVHW011519210220
647795LV00012B/635